W9-BIO-367

South Bend Public Library
South Bend, Indiana
Gift Book
Presented by
ANONYMOUS DONOR

How to Put
POWER
and
DIRECTION
in Your Golf

How to Put *POWER* *and* *DIRECTION* in Your Golf

by

JOE NOVAK

Instructor
Bel Air Country Club
Los Angeles, California

NEW YORK : 1954
PRENTICE-HALL, INC.

 Printed in the United States of America. L.C. Card Number: 54-6852.

Dedication

Dedicated to the countless many in both professional and amateur ranks, who, by their approval and commendation, stimulated me to do this second book on golf—with the hope that it will give the reader more enjoyment and improved accomplishment through a better understanding of the game.

Contents

Introduction

"WHY ANOTHER BOOK ON GOLF?" THIS QUESTION HAS OFTEN BEEN ASKED.

I think there is a good reason for "another" golf book—I have written a golf book that contains a formula, that presents a definite plan of action, a routine. This book establishes a system by which any player can readily learn the knack of good golf. It is a book with a plan and a conclusion.

I have tried to convey three things:

First, that golf is an easy game to learn and an easy game to play.

Second, that all good golfers do exactly the same things—they follow a set pattern.

Third, that to play A-1 golf all you have to do is master two things.

Let me explain these three points.

Point 1. Golf Is Easy

No one can deny that golf is an easy game to play. There are no restrictions as to time or method of making a shot. Furthermore, the ball is sitting still, waiting for the player to hit it. There is no deceptive delivery of the ball and no one interferes in any way with the player's swing. The player is permitted full use of various types of clubs. These clubs are designed to produce different shots.

For example, if a golfer wants to produce a long, low drive he selects a club designed to do just that—he selects a driver. If the player must lift his ball over a tree or wants to loft it over a brook or a sand trap, he uses a club designed for that specific shot—he uses a No. 5 iron.

For distance, the player has a choice of a set of drivers, for lifting the ball over obstacles or onto the green he has a set of "lofters" or irons. Finally, when the player has played his ball into position for the final purpose—onto the green for a shot at the cup—he uses still another type of club. He uses a putter, a club designed to roll the ball.

This classification of clubs shows that in golf there are three kinds of play: (1) drives or long shots that test the player's power or ability to "get distance"; (2) approach shots produced with specially designed clubs that lift and drop the ball to the desired position; and (3) putts, or shots that get the ball into the cup.

No, golf is not, for example, like tennis. In tennis the player is armed only with one "club" and he must produce a variety of effects by executing different strokes. But the golfer—well, all he has to do in order to get the shot he wants is to select a club and "let the club do the work." And what is more, the golfer does not change his swing or stroke as he switches from one club to another. *He uses exactly the same swing all the way through the game.*

Point 2. All Good Golfers Do the Same Thing

There is a uniform pattern that all good golfers employ. A study of the top tournament performers will, of course, show slight variations in style, but the winners, the "champions," all perform in precisely the same way.

A study of the form of Bobby Jones, Gene Sarazen, Ben Hogan,

Sam Snead, Byron Nelson—all in the top bracket as champions—reveals that they have a definite uniformity of style. Unfortunately, there is some feeling that no two golfers play alike nor can any two golfers be taught alike.

A few years ago I arranged to give a series of twelve golf lessons on the radio. On hearing of the plan a friend of mine said, "What's all this I hear about your giving golf lessons on the radio?"

"Nothing at all," I said. "It's all set to start next week."

"But," my friend objected, "I don't understand how you can possibly teach golf over the *radio*."

"Why not?" I answered. "They teach cooking, they teach Spanish, they teach piano over the air. Why can't I teach golf?"

"Yes," he said, "I understand they're doing all those things. But how can you teach golf when everybody needs a different kind of swing?"

There are many golfers who have just that notion. They seem to get the idea that because they are tall, or short, or thin, or thick, they should have a special swing designed just for them!

If such were the case, we would be giving in to the player's weakness, instead of outlining the basic requirement of good golf and then helping the player combat whatever weaknesses may appear.

Point 3. There Are Only Two Things to Learn in Golf

I hope that I've made my first two points clear—that it is not only possible but that it is practical to use the same swing all the way through on *all* shots, and that all good golfers use this same swing—no matter what club they use.

It is simply a case of "let the club do the work." Obviously the only way to get the true effect of the clubs is to use them all in exactly the same way.

Considering the results desired in a golf shot, we can see that a golfer needs only two things: *Power* (or distance) and *Direction.*

If a golfer can hit his shots *far enough* and *straight enough* there are no problems.

But what are the controlling factors in power and direction? And how can power and direction be developed?

In this book I will show you that power and direction are easy to acquire and easy to retain.

A study of all the golfers in the world will readily reveal that they belong in one of two categories: *those who play golf* or *those who play at it.* Further study would reveal that whether they "play golf" or "play at it" is determined by one thing: *All good golfers have a sense of body control (or pivot) with which they actually execute the swing.*

Inability to use this body control forces the player to swing the club with his arms and hands—a poor substitute for the real swing, which is done with the body turn or pivot. There is nothing new or startling in this idea of body turn—it is a common performance in all sports.

In all sports, regardless of whether the player wants to impart energy through his hands or his feet, it is essential that a turning or pivotal action of the body is used to develop that force. At the same time this pivot takes place, there is footwork or shift of weight so that the necessary body turn can be made. The basis of a good golf swing lies entirely in this sense of body control, but this body control requires the proper footwork. Once the golfer learns to use his legs properly, he is well on his way to executing the correct shot.

Only one more thing needs to be added to make the golf shot a success. It is one thing to be able to develop the power, but it is still another thing to impart this power to the club.

Players readily grasp the need of footwork and body action, but for various reasons the action of the hands as they impart this energy to the club continues to be with many golfers an unfound art. There are many reasons why this hand action cannot be understood readily by everyone, and I would like at this time to digress for a moment to review briefly some of the teaching methods in use in this country.

Erroneous teaching methods have developed faulty habits that should be eliminated in order to get a simple idea of the execution of the golf shot.

Early books on golf all had a definite outline. Chapter one was on the driver; chapter two was on the brassie; three was on the spoon; four on the driving iron; and so on down through all the clubs. Naturally this created the impression that each club was handled differently. And this notion still prevails in the minds of many.

I have seen instructors teach in this manner. The pupil is started with a few lessons on the driver. He is then advanced to the long-iron shots, then to the short-iron shots, then to the chip shots. In this way he acquires the notion that each club is handled differently. Then, finally, he is brought to the green, and the instructor, having run out of ideas and strokes, says, "Now putting is something that cannot be taught. Putters are born, not made. Assume a comfortable position and do your best."

This, of course, is ridiculous. Putting can be taught just the same as any other part of the game. Putting requires a sense of direction and the ability to gauge the necessary power to sink the putt. And these can be taught.

A second "school" of instruction, perhaps a continental influence from the private tutor regimes, was based on the theory that no two persons have the same build, therefore each person must have an individual golf swing designed to suit him. This type of instruction creates a tendency to cater to the individual's weaknesses, whereas the more simple and effective plan is to prescribe the requirements and then let the pupil conform to them.

The third and perhaps most widely used method of instruction is the type that theorizes that the player must not use his body in any way in the execution of a golf shot. Oh, yes—when using a full shot the player may be allowed to turn slightly during his swing, but certainly there is to be no body movement in the execution of the iron shots, and of course for short shots and putting it is a complete case of *rigor mortis.*

Such a theory develops, of course, an unusual amount of wrist and hand action because the hands and wrists are about all there is to swing the club with. Except in very "ladylike" half-shots such a procedure proves ineffective in getting distance or maintaining direction.

With all these schools of instruction it is no wonder that there is a conflict of ideas in golf! This book is an effort to eliminate some of this confusion; an effort to show that golf is an easy game to play, that there is a club for every kind of shot, and all the player has to do is to swing it.

In well over thirty years of teaching I have found only one method that will produce satisfactory results. That is to break up the swing into segments and then step-by-step lead the pupil through the routine until the whole thing becomes a perfectly smooth, natural procedure. And this step by step procedure naturally calls for numbers that can automatically identify and properly time the movements. The simple 1-2-3-4 rhythm of taking the correct position and the 1-2-3-4 rhythm of making the swing has proved helpful to many golfers.

We will attempt now in this book to explain these basic movements through words and pictures. All of the sequence pictures in the book were made by Tad Gillam, Los Angeles, and his "Miracle Eye" camera, and they—together with the vivid lessons to be learned from studying the three-dimensional pictures—will help any golfer to put power and direction in his golf game.

ONE

Grip, Stance, and Balance

EVERY GOLF SHOT IS A STORY IN TWO PARTS—"GETTING SET" IS THE introduction to the tale, and the "swing" is its conclusion. All golfers should remember the time-worn slogan, "Well begun is half done," because the preliminaries to a shot go far toward determining its effectiveness.

Before getting into the three basic movements of the golf shot—good footwork, body pivot, and hand action—which make up the swing, we must concern ourselves with getting set correctly. This requires a good understanding of the proper grip, stance, and balance, all mighty important ingredients to a good golfer.

Grip, stance, and balance are the equivalent of taking aim, and only when they are executed in the correct manner is the golfer ready to proceed to pull the trigger in the swing, the second half of his shot. There is nothing more graceful, nothing as easy and natural, as the correct golf swing, but a player cannot hope to attain the goal of a good swing until he has a definite understanding of how to get set in a comfortable, natural position.

Confidence comes with knowledge. This is a good thing to remember when considering the mental aspect of the game, which is peculiarly important in golf.

Golf is one of the few games played with a "still" ball. The little white sphere just sits there, waiting for the player to do something about it. If a player does not work out some definite plan of action and know exactly what he will do, mental bogies and confused situations can, and generally do, arise.

In most other sports the ball is in motion, and the player must possess some natural ability to get into position and execute the desired result. If the shot or play is missed, he often can pass off the result with the excuse that he wasn't ready. He keeps on playing and missing, but no one gets excited about it unless his performance is so bad that he cannot "make the team." If this is the case, he often just gives up the whole thing as a bad job.

Golf is different. *There is no excuse for missing a shot.* The player has his choice of clubs to use on each shot, he can take just about as long as he wants to get ready, and he can do just as he pleases in hitting the ball. With all of this latitude and freedom, it's no wonder that a golfer can become annoyed and frustrated if his shots don't come off easily and naturally.

When he is not organized properly at the start, a player may contradict himself muscularly, increasing confusion to a point where neither mind nor muscle can function, and the execution of the shot seemingly becomes impossible.

Tension and confusion can be eliminated in a very short time by following an orderly four-step routine, which makes the correct

1 2 3

starting position automatic. Then, by employing a second 1-2-3-4 pattern, the swing follows naturally and correctly.

Let's study the first four steps, so we can take correct aim in the right attitude. The enthusiasm and aggressiveness that should be present will add to the natural fun of accomplishment as we strive to do better on each shot.

Placing the Club to the Ball

The *first step* is to place the club behind the ball with the left hand. When placing the club to the ball, the player should make sure the club handle is tilted slightly forward in the direction of the shot. There should be a feeling of having the club turned down on the ball, as if the golfer were going to drive the ball into the ground. The club should not be tilted as though it were going to scoop the ball up into the air.

The left hand should be well toward the top of the club, with the thumb behind the club shaft. The thumb should apply a pressure at the back of the club handle, in the direction of the shot's path.

No matter what grip is used in Step No. 1, it should be a very light one, confined to the first two fingers and thumb. In other words, the grip is restricted to the front part of the hand—not the back of the hand, as is often recommended. But we'll discuss the grip later on. For now, just be sure that the left arm is in a comfortable, natural position, not stiff, extended, or rigid.

Getting the Feet in Position

Proper position of the feet is of the utmost importance. The golfer always should place the left foot opposite the ball, so that a line running from the ball to the left heel will be at a right angle to the intended line of the shot.

The right foot is placed so that the toes of both feet are on a line parallel to the line of the shot. The position described is known as the *square stance.* If the right foot is placed slightly forward of a line parallel to the line of the shot, the resulting position is called an *open stance.* The open stance should be used only when the player is deliberately playing a slice. By moving the right foot in the opposite direction, that is, farther away from the ball, the player is taking a *closed stance.* The closed stance is useful when the golfer wishes to make a hook shot, curving the ball to the left. Hooking and slicing will be explained in another chapter.

Remember that the left foot always should be opposite the ball, and a line running from the ball to the left heel should form a right angle with the line of the shot. A later discussion will explain more fully why the ball should be lined up in this manner, and point out the exceptions to the rule. To review, in Step No. 1 the club was placed behind the ball using the left arm only, and in Step No. 2 the left foot was lined up opposite the ball and the right foot placed on a line parallel to the line of the shot.

The feet should not be too far apart. If there is any doubt in the player's mind, he should keep his feet close together. Good golf requires good body pivot on all shots, and good body pivot cannot be done very easily from a wide stance. At no time should the feet be spread to a point wider than the shoulders. On very short shots, the heels should be quite close together.

It might be well to observe at this time that a perfectly normal

4 5 6

foot position would be to have both feet pointed outward, but only very slightly.

Completing the Grip

At this point, the weight is evenly divided on both feet. The right hand is nowhere near the club, and it will be found that it cannot be brought over to the club without relaxing the right knee and allowing the right side to turn very slightly toward the ball.

As the right hand is brought to the club, it is brought over as though it were going to slap forward in the direction of the shot. Now, as the hand reaches the club it assumes a position on the club shaft that is directly opposite to that of the left hand. The left hand is on top of the club handle, and the right hand assumes a position underneath the club handle.

It was suggested that the grip for the left hand be confined to the forepart of the hand, and this same procedure should be followed with the right hand.

The Overlapping Grip

It will be found that the last or little finger of each hand is not needed for the grip. This naturally will permit the hands to be brought closely together on the club—the right hand actually will close over the left hand one finger—that is, the little finger of the right hand will overlap the forefinger of the left hand. The left thumb will fit automatically into the hollow of the right hand, and a perfect sense of opposition between the hands should develop from this formation. As the right hand tends to pull, the left hand tends to oppose, so that a natural pull-and-push effect is developed between the hands.

This position of the hands on the club is known as the *overlapping grip,* and it is the grip used by practically every golf star today. Of course, there are exceptions to the rule, although one of our great American golf heroes, Francis Ouimet, recently decided to change from the interlocking to the overlapping grip. Curiously, Gene Sarazen, who once stated that he felt he would have played much more effectively with the overlapping grip, started playing golf when Ouimet, then 19 years old, had just tied with two great British players, Harry Vardon and Ted Ray, for the U.S. Open Golf Championship. Using the interlocking grip, Ouimet proceeded to beat Vardon and Ray in a historic playoff, an event which did much to popularize golf in this country. Naturally, Sarazen copied the hero's grip. It is interesting to note, too, that the winner of the 1952 U.S. Open, Julius Boros, of Mid-Pines Country Club, North Carolina, also uses the interlocking grip.

The Interlocking Grip

Although I do not recommend the interlocking grip, it is described here to show how it differs from the overlapping grip. In the interlocking grip, the little finger of the right hand is interlaced with the forefinger of the left hand. Such a grip has a tendency to concentrate a tension in the back part of each hand, making proper handling of the club a difficult task. Only an expert can use this grip successfully.

Returning to Step No. 3, let me remind you that the player must be sure to use the overlapping grip, letting the little finger of the

7 8 9

right hand overlap the forefinger of the left hand. The right hand cannot be brought to the club without relaxing the right knee slightly, and as the right knee relaxes, the weight of the body must be shifted to the left foot, so that the player actually assumes an off-center position. At the end of Step No. 3, most of the weight is on the left foot, and this is exactly the position the player should be in when his club is meeting the ball in the shot.

Getting the Proper Balance

Left-handed people prefer to stand on the left foot and right-handed people are more comfortable when balancing on the right foot, due to the fact that we are all built like the letter *X*. That is, the right foot and right leg work with the left arm and the left hand, and vice versa, in a sort of criss-cross action across the body. This can be demonstrated in the following manner: Place your *right* foot and *right* shoulder against a wall and then raise your *left* foot off the floor—or reverse the procedure and raise your right foot off the floor. In either case, you will lose your balance and tend to fall.

In 9 cases out of 10, the average player actually immobilizes himself as he gets ready to make a golf shot. He has the idea that when he gets ready to start the swing his weight should be evenly divided on both feet, balancing him for the swing. Nothing could be further from the proper procedure.

Some girls, inexperienced athletically, find it difficult to throw a ball because they try to throw with the arm only, not having acquired the knack of getting the feet into proper position. In a recent opening ball game on the Pacific Coast, movie star Zsa Zsa Gabor was to throw the first pitch. When she attempted to throw the ball across home plate, Zsa Zsa was amazed to see the ball travel to third base instead! She just didn't use her feet and body correctly, and wasn't in position to make the throw.

The golfer who plants himself on both feet, distributing his weight evenly between them, is doomed to failure from the start, because he is actually locking himself in a set position. The feet and legs are important in almost every sport, as evidenced by the old saying, "Ballplayers and boxers are through when their legs are gone."

Turning the Right Heel Out

It was pointed out at the end of Step No. 2 that the natural foot position is one where both feet are pointed slightly outward. At the end of Step No. 3, the feet are still in this position. Now, in Step No. 4, turn the right heel out slightly, just enough to have the right foot at a right angle to the line of the shot. This very slight movement of the right foot can be most helpful. A golf club is swung with a pivot motion of the body, and in the swing, weight and feet must be right.

If the player assumes a position where both feet are pointed outward in an extreme manner, he will be locking the hips and actually preventing correct body motion.

After the club is placed to the ball with the left hand, the feet placed in position, and the right hand brought to the club to complete the grip, we carry out Step No. 4, turning the right heel out slightly. Because turning the right heel outward actually widens the stance, it can be seen now why it is much better to start with a narrow or close foot position. It does away with the danger of acquiring too wide a stance, which would be a detriment to the full, free body pivot a golfer should develop.

This slight outward turn requires a little practice, but it gives the player a sense of freedom throughout the right hip. It also gives a more secure position of the right foot at the top of the swing, where steadiness is a necessity.

Johnny McHugh, a great amateur player from San Francisco, used to flip both heels outward before the swing. This action is found in many other sports—many baseball and football players employ this "pigeon-toed" stance to make themselves more free and mobile, ready to meet any type of action from any direction.

By doing this right heel flip, the player will find that he can turn more readily, more fully, and more steadily, and, to use an old golfing term, it will be easier for him to "come back on the inside"—but more of that later.

Summary of Steps 1-4

A study of the results of the first four steps, or the completed position, reveals the following:

a. The player is balanced on his left foot.

b. His body is slightly turned toward the direction of the shot, so that he is "leaning against the club."

c. While the left foot remains in a position where it is turned slightly outward, the right foot is at a right angle to the line of the shot, this right foot position giving an added feeling of being able to lean against the ball.

d. The feet are fairly close together, not in a wide stance.

e. The left hand is on top of the club shaft, and the right hand is in an opposing position behind and under the club.

f. The hands are not tense and tight on the club but are relaxed, with a definite feeling of grip confined to the first two fingers and the thumbs of each hand.

g. The right arm is relaxed, and the relaxed feeling is noticeable also in the left arm, with a definite akimbo feeling at the elbows.

This position of the arms is a help in creating the sense of opposition that should always be present in the hands, something which a very straight left arm position does not impart to most people.

All of these points are important and could be termed essential, but now the player must acquire the knack of getting them all lined up properly. Individually these points really mean nothing—they are just so much information. The real objective is to develop a working arrangement between feet, hands, and body. Only by following and repeating a plan or pattern can this objective be reached and getting "lined up" become an easy habit.

If a golfer consistently follows the four steps we have described, the correct position can be established almost overnight.

STEP NO. 1: Place the club behind the ball with the left hand.
STEP NO. 2: Place the feet in position.
STEP NO. 3: Complete the grip by relaxing the right knee.
STEP NO. 4: Turn the right heel out.

This pattern automatically gets feet, hands, and body properly lined up. Practice until it becomes a habit, and then you will be ready to start in with the actual stroke in another series of four steps.

TWO

The Full Swing with the Driver

A GOLF SWING IS A GOLF SWING, REGARDLESS OF THE CLUB THAT IS BEING used. Whether it is a full swing or a short swing, the golf swing requires the same degree of coordination, the same knack of combining the various operations of feet, hands, and body into the desired objective of power and direction, in every case. Inasmuch as the illustrations in this chapter are of a full swing with the driver, I shall explain in words and demonstrate with pictures just exactly *what* takes place, *when* it occurs, and *how* it is done.

The various examples and discussions in this book are for the

10 11 12

purpose of clarifying certain ideas on golf and proving certain contentions of the author, contentions he has found to be true in his years of teaching the game. While theory and discussion are necessary to establish a clear understanding, the practical purpose of this book is to teach players how to improve their game and reduce their score by giving them a definite plan of procedure.

Imitation vs. Rules

One of the most annoying comments heard in golf often comes from a player who has just won a tournament. The new champion very likely will state that he "never had a lesson in his life." Maybe he did not actually take formal lessons, but he did learn from observation, and the person he imitated is entitled to some credit.

I contend that there are just two ways to learn to play golf—entirely by *imitation,* which is the way most of our champions have acquired the knack of playing good golf, and by *rule.* Because they do play by imitation, from model, and from memory, the champions don't bother to reason or analyze. They just play! This often leads to temperament because, if and when the "feel" leaves them, they just don't know exactly how to get back on the track, and they get a bit temperamental.

13 14 15

The only other way to learn to play golf is to follow the method being advanced in this book—that is, to play by rule. Establish a pattern or a plan and stick to the rules that constitute that pattern or plan.

In recent years there has been a tendency in golf instruction to advance the idea that "everything goes together," and that the player should think of a golf swing as a one-piece movement—this makes it all so simple, they say. I cannot subscribe to such a theory. There are certain basic things that must be done in a golf shot, and the player cannot simplify the procedure by just closing his eyes to the requirements.

I believe that with a definite, orderly pattern, the execution of a

16 17 18

19 20 21

golf shot can become easy, clear, and simple. And a thing is not simple unless it is completely and entirely understood.

Assuming that the player has learned how to take his aim and, by practicing the first four steps has learned the stance, the grip, and the body position, let's proceed to outline the requirements of the swing and then, by another 1-2-3-4 routine, learn how to get the knack and rhythm of the actual golf swing.

The Pivot and Swing

It is important to remember that a golf club is swung by the action of the body. The idea of pivot control, while quite common

22 23 24

25 26 27

today, is really a fairly modern concept. While I do not set myself up as an expert on the matter, I feel that the success of our American golfers in British golf championships is the result of the more powerful type of game our golfers all seem to play. Our players, perhaps from the influence of baseball, are all inclined to "put their backs into it" and try for a home run, whereas the British, under the influence of their national game, cricket, are inclined to just "lay the bat on the ball."

When Bobby Jones first went to England to play, I distinctly remember he was criticized because he played a certain hole with a drive and a No. 6 iron, when the proper way to play the hole was with a drive and a spoon. Let me say that I find nothing wrong with the play and performances of Britain's star players. In fact, I feel that though they are tremendously outnumbered by the American tournament troupers, the British players do present real competition today.

The early books on golf did not lay much stress or emphasis on body control, but it is rather significant to note that several recent golf volumes give this phase of the game more than passing mention.

Some years ago, while teaching golf to a 45-year-old gentleman, the author was criticized by one of the more experienced club members for the manner of instruction he was using. The critic had been a former eastern state champion and the winner of many tournaments. He felt that the method being used was not the proper procedure for an older pupil. The whole discussion revolved around the subject of body motion. The dissenter thought that the author had his pupil using his body too much and there was too much swaying and lateral movement during the swing. He was one of those golfers who insists that there be no excessive body action. The instructor advised the critic that he could improve his own game if he would mend his ways and learn to pivot on the short iron shots—it would probably help him to stop shanking his approach shots, which he was prone to do at times.

But this golfer was quite set in his ways, and his game went from a one-time 4 handicap to a 21 handicap. While age naturally had something to do with his loss of golf efficiency, this man's refusal to pivot purposely on any shot probably was an important factor. By comparison, my pupil, within a period of five years, toned down his excessive swaying and went on to win the club championship.

I cite these two cases as proof that older players can find the game more enjoyable and less exerting if they get their PGA instructor to give them proper guidance on the need and value of pivoting.

In no shot in golf is pivoting as important as it is in the short approach shot and putting. Of course, golfers readily admit the need for body turn in a tee shot or a wood shot from the fairway, but they do not seem to realize the need for body motion in other

28

29

30

31

32

33

shots. Why are so many putts being hooked to the left of the cup? Why do so many golfers shank their short approach shots? The errors in both cases are definitely due to lack of proper body motion.

The correct pivot cannot be made unless one understands correct footwork. Many golfers fail to recognize the golf swing as actually being two swings in one. There is an upswing or backswing, which carries the club up, and a downswing, which carries the club down and through.

In order to carry the club up or to the right, the player must be on his right foot, and to carry the club down, he must be on his left foot. No one can make any sort of a decent pivot motion on the backswing while he keeps his weight on the left foot, nor can he follow through naturally if he keeps his weight on the right foot as he swings through.

One of the major difficulties people have in playing golf comes from a lack of understanding of the simple, natural sense of pivoting. Pivoting is present everywhere, even in the everyday activity of walking. Analyze it. A person does not walk solely with his legs. He balances himself on one leg and then pivots on that leg to place the other leg in a forward position. Once that leg is forward, the person balances himself on it, and it becomes the pivot leg while the other leg swings forward.

Pivoting in a golf shot is just as simple as pivoting in walking. The player must balance himself on his right foot and right leg so that he can pivot to the right for the upswing. Then he must shift his weight and balance himself on his left leg in order to pivot a second time for the downswing, thereby bringing the club down and through the ball. A player can move the club back and forth freely, easily, and naturally only when he understands the principle of shifting the weight from one foot to the other so that the respective pivots can be made.

Many golfers do not realize that it is one thing to shift the weight and another to pivot. Many try to do it all together, but that is impossible. The dictionary defines the word "pivot" as "the rotation of a mass on an axis." Pivoting is simple if one will distinguish the axis from the rotation. I remember an instance when an instructor was trying desperately to get his pupil to turn more on the backswing. "Imagine, please," he beseeched, "that you have a spike driven from your right shoulder, through your right side, down to your right heel, and then please turn your entire left side as though you were opening a gate." That is just about how that operation worked—like a gate, and a rusty one.

The Upswing

On the upswing, the pivot is simple and natural. Shift the weight to the right foot and then take the club back to the right as if you were getting ready to throw it. The upswing is a motion similar to the wind-up preparatory to throwing a ball. With the weight on the right foot, a natural drawing back by the right hip draws the right arm back into a cocked position. As the arm is drawn back, the left knee raises and kicks almost straight forward in order to balance this backward movement of the right arm.

The Downswing

As the club is started on its way down, the weight must be shifted to the left foot, and when that axis is established, a backward pull

34

35

36

of the left hip pulls the left arm down and through. As the arm is pulled down, through the action of the left side, the right knee is kicked up and forward to maintain a balance on the axis.

These movements should be tried and practiced without a club. Simply let the arms hang naturally and let the action of the right side carry them to the top of the swing. Then allow the action of the left side to bring them down and through the swing.

Footwork and body motion are so dependent upon each other, and in time they work so smoothly, that some golfers are inclined to believe that they are one and the same movement. But they are not. It is one thing to shift the weight to establish an axis, but rotating on that axis is another matter. This combination of footwork and body pivot constitute the basis of the golf swing, and the pivot generates the energy or force which is applied to the club.

The Hands

One remaining factor to be considered is how to transmit or apply the power we have generated with this body movement to the club through the hands. All we have to do is coordinate the action of the hands with the motion of the body, and this, too, is a very simple matter.

All muscles contract or expand, depending upon the movement of the limbs. Arms contract and expand. With the pulling back of the right side, the right arm is contracted and the left arm is then free to extend or expand. As the right arm contracts, it pulls on the club, and as the left arm expands or extends itself, it pushes on the club. This push-and-pull action of the arms and hands becomes the very crux of the golf swing.

Now that we have developed good footwork and a responsive, coordinated pivot action of the body with which to swing the club, another problem arises as the club is being swung up on the backswing and continues on through the downswing. That problem is in knowing the position of the club while it is being swung. The swing is accomplished with the body and arms, but it is important to know just where the club is during the swing. Just as a billiard player deliberately cocks his cue up or down on the cue ball, a golfer can cock his club in or out, so that an intentional hook or slice is produced.

This operation is done entirely with the hands. However, every golfer must learn to control the swing of the club with his body and arms before his hands are free to give him positional control of the club. We are not losing sight of the importance of the body pivot. The power comes from the body turn, but the directional aspect of the shot is basically dependent upon the action of the hands, so they are equally important in any golf shot. These two actions, involving the body and the hands, must be synchronized, or the shot will fail in its objective. This is just as true in an 8-foot putt as it is in a 250-yard drive.

All good golfers have this combination of "body for *power,* hands for *direction.*" While there is a certain knack about it, there is no secret or mystery about golf. It is a logical combination of certain necessary movements.

It is through the hands that the player gets the sense of feel; it is with the hands that the player actually cocks or sets the club; it is with the hands that the player keeps the club in position throughout the swing; and it is through the hands that the power of the body

37 38 39

pivot flows into the club. Therefore, the action of the hands is extremely important.

Because the hands have so much to do in golf, there are many conflicting ideas about how they should work in the swing. The fairly recent ideas about hand action in the golf shot are (1) the right hand should start the club from the ball at the outset of the backswing, and (2) the so-called wrist action or set of the club should be made early in the backswing, instead of at the top of the swing.

Watch any good golfer as he prepares to make a golf shot, and this is what he will do: *After taking careful stance and grip position, he invariably gives the club a distinctive wiggle and then suddenly flips it about 24 inches from the ball.* This process may be repeated one, two, four, or even more times, after which the player again will place the club down to the ball. Suddenly, before you know it, the club is up and down and the shot is on its way.

Let's analyze just what the golfer did. First he wiggled the club handle back and forth as the club remained on the ground behind the ball. This was done to get a certain sense of footwork or proper weight shift. Then the clubhead was flipped away from the ball about 24 inches and returned again. This was done to get the feel of the club in the hands, and more important, to get the feel of just how the club was going to be cocked or set with the hands before it was swung back and then forward with the pivot action of the body. This is a perfectly logical procedure. The player should feel right and steady on his feet. He should know, through his hands, where the club is, and only then can he turn on the power from his body. Only when the two preliminary steps have been accomplished do good golfers actually "haul off" in the swing itself, which is, as Bobby Jones so aptly expressed, something that starts within you.

After the weight has been shifted to the right foot, and the hands cock the club into position, a body pivot on the right foot and then a reverse pivot on the left foot bring the club up into the backswing and down through the ball. Before we get into the detail of just how to do this, step by step, I would like to give you several examples of the importance of the hand action in golf.

Direction through Hand Action

At a recent tournament players' meeting in Chicago, plans were being discussed for improving the tournaments. Jackie Burke, a leading money winner and one of our younger stars, requested sponsors to clip their course fairways very short, even though the grass may tend to dry up and take away that nice, green, lush look all golf course chairmen want their courses to have. When pressed for the reason for his request, Burke explained that tournament players cannot put any "stuff" on the ball or play any extraordinary shots unless the ball is lying fairly "clean." This type of shot requires a fine sense of club action, and this depends greatly on the hands.

Here is another example of the importance of using the hands to get the feel of the club. Quite some time ago, a star player made up his mind to win a certain tournament, regardless of the time or annoyance he caused other participants. He stepped up on the first tee and very carefully waggled his club, not twice, not four times, not eight times, but twenty times before he swung at the ball! He continued this excessive waggling of the club, causing much irritation among his playing partners. Keeping up the procedure, he refused to haul off into his swing until he was good and ready. The result was a 68, a new course record! He wiggled and waggled his club through the second day, and again broke the course record with a 67, to lead the field at this point by 7 shots.

By now he had lost any friendly playing partners he may have had, and his procedure delayed play so much that the committee called him in and objected to the tedious playing. Being a good sport, he agreed to play faster the next day, and he did. He stepped up to the ball and, without an appreciable wiggle, hauled off and played his shots. His score was 81, fourteen strokes worse than the previous day! On the last round he finished with a 77 to wind up in seventh place, far away from the first prize of $3500.

The point of the story is this: *The player was getting the proper feel of his club through instinct.* By wiggling and waggling his club, he would finally get it where he wanted before making his shot. When the committee asked him to play faster, he was like a ship without a rudder, just swinging away, not really knowing the exact position of the club before he made the swing.

I am not suggesting that you follow this player's procedure, but the story will emphasize the importance of knowing how to use your hands so that you know where the club is at all times.

One of my pupils complained about lack of distance in his shots. When it was pointed out that his stance was so wide he could not pivot and was merely using his hands, he tried a narrower stance and immediately began hitting longer shots. But a slice developed, and he asked what was causing it. I told him that his club was out of position, that the clubface was open, causing it to cut across the ball. To correct his difficulty, I advised him to break his wrists just as he started his club away from the ball. Before I could finish, my pupil broke in, "I've been playing golf for thirty years, and I always break my wrists at the top of the swing. Now you want me to change!"

I knew my friend did a lot of duck hunting. I asked him, "What do you do when you hunt—do you pull the trigger, then aim, or do you aim and then pull the trigger?" I think he got the point.

Another time I was doing my best to teach a beginner how to play golf, and in a short time he got the knack of shifting his weight and soon had a good-looking swing. But he, too, developed a slice. I explained to him the necessity of proper club positioning at the outset of the backswing, showing him how cocking the club open produced a slice and cocking it closed caused a hook. He responded by saying, "Joe, I don't want to know how to hook or slice. I just want to know how to hit them straight."

But, you can't hit them straight until you learn to cock your club in the correct position, and the hook and slice technique are the only guides one has to reach that correct position. A golfer must recognize this fact if he wants to make any progress.

I'm glad to say that the disappointments are far overshadowed by the success of other pupils who are willing to put some effort into improving their game. One of my friends had a handicap of 10, and he became alarmed when his handicap went to 13. Upon analyzing his game, we found that his footwork was excellent, that he had a fine pivot action with his body, but his hand action was definitely bad. Within a short time after correcting this fault, the player scored a 66, 4 under par. A while later his handicap dropped to 3, where it has remained for several years—which means that he consistently scores in the low 70's. Recently he made two hole-in-ones within a month, and on another occasion he scored a 29 for nine holes, 7 under par! Just more proof that the hands are all-important in golf.

A somewhat humorous phase of the hand action in golf came about when another player requested a golf lesson. I had no idea he would immediately enter a golf game after the instruction, joining a group of strangers who were much better golfers. Like many others, this golfer wanted to play before he had fully conquered his problems. At any rate, he drew Reginald Owen, the famous actor, as a partner. When the guest became rather confused in his new company, and a bit more perplexed with his golf technique, Owen stepped over to him and said, "My poor man, what are you trying to do?"

40 41 42

The guest answered, "I just took a golf lesson from Joe Novak, and I'm trying to break my wrist."

"Break your wrist!" said Reggie. "You bloody well better stop playing so well or you'll break my pocketbook!"

So much for the theory and analysis of the values of footwork, pivot, and hands. Let's now take up the proper procedure in the execution of a golf shot. In the first four steps, the player (1) *places the club behind the ball with his left hand,* (2) *places the feet in proper position,* (3) *completes the grip by bringing the right hand to the club,* and (4) *turns the right heel out.*

After the first four steps, the golfer should find himself in the following position:

a. Standing with ball opposite the left foot.
b. Weight balanced on left foot.
c. Feet fairly close toether.
d. Left hand definitely on top of club.
e. Right hand in opposing position to left hand.
f. Hands and arms relaxed.

Now we are ready to go on to the next four steps, which will take us through the actual swing. But before going on to page 46, let's take a close look at the full swing with the aid of the 3-D pictures on the following pages.

How to Look at the 3-D Pictures

In the envelope attached to the inside front cover you will find your 3-D glasses. Remove the glasses from the envelope and hold them, as directed, in your *right* hand. The next four pages show you, in three dimensions, the complete swing. View the pictures in a good, strong light, and you will find that by moving the book you can see down *into* the pictures and see the actual angle of the arms, body, and club.

3-D Picture 1—Address to the Ball

Because my arms and the club shaft are not in a stiff, straight line, my arms hang naturally—comfortably—to meet the club handle. My hands are also opposite each other. Look down into the picture and you will see my left hand on top of the club and my right hand just about underneath the shaft. I am balanced on my left foot. You will be in this same position when your club meets the ball at the time of impact.

3-D Picture 2—The Top of the Swing

Watch my left and right hands—apparently relaxed, but really balanced to keep the club in a steady position. I am poised on my right foot—the angle of my knee will stand out through your glasses. This is a rather straight, forward position. I prefer it to the one in which the left knee is turned sideways toward the right toe.

3-D Picture 3—Just Before Impact with the Ball

Just before my club meets the ball I am well balanced on my left foot. A pull-back action of my left hip causes a natural coordination between my right knee and my left arm. My right hand and arm are giving support. The muscles standing out on my two hands show that golf is definitely a game in which both hands must always work together.

Special Note: This position of the club—just before impact—is an exact reproduction of the position created at the beginning of the upswing. It is at this point in the upswing—just before or just as the body exerts its influence in actually swinging the club up—that you should establish the desired position of the club. Study the chapter on "Hands" in connection with this picture. It presents the desired position in both the up- and the downswing at this exact point.

3-D Picture 4—The Follow Through

My body has natural balance on my left foot for the follow through. The full sweep of the club shows that my left arm couldn't help giving the ball a natural backhanded application, while my right hand and arm gave a steady supporting base throughout the entire downswing.

The Forward Press

The first move in the swing is known as the *forward press.* In the preliminary position (see page 39), the player is balanced on his left foot. As long as he remains in that position, it is impossible to carry the club to the right or away from the ball. He is "leaning against the ball," and this is exactly the position he will be in when the club is striking the ball in the swing. The player is really leaning in one direction when he wants to move the club in the opposite direction, but this is all part of the pattern.

To get out of this preliminary position and start his swing, the player employs the one-two motion of footwork, two moves which are carried out without taking the club off the ground. Without raising the right heel, he makes a forward motion of the right knee. This forward motion prompts the player then to reverse his knee position, thereby transferring his weight to the right leg. In Step No. 1 of this one-two motion, the hands are swung over past the left knee as the right knee moves forward. In Step No. 2, the hands swing back past the ball and are nearly opposite the right knee as the weight is shifted to the right leg.

The clubhead has remained on the ground during the one-two motion of the forward press (Step No. 1 and Step No. 2). *But the face of the club does not remain square with the ball; it is actually open on Step No. 1 and closed on Step No. 2.* In addition to the weight shift from the left foot to the right foot in the forward press, there is a shift in the control of the club handle. Control of the club is in the left hand on Step No. 1, and it shifts to the right hand on Step No. 2.

The Backswing

With his weight on the right foot as the result of Steps No. 1 and 2, the golfer now is ready to take the clubhead off the ground to start the backswing, Step No. 3. The right hand starts to pick the

43

44

45

club up off the ground as if it were going to be placed on the player's right hip. Almost simultaneously, the left hand, principally through the left thumb, begins to oppose this upward motion, and a natural downward thrust of the left hand kicks the club into a set or fixed position. With the upward pick-up of the right hand and the opposing downward thrust of the left hand, the club can be kicked into any one of three positions, depending upon the direction the left hand moves.

The Hook and the Slice. If in the pick-up action of the right hand and the downward thrust of the left hand the left wrist and hand turn outwardly and away from the body, the club is kicked into a closed position. That is, the face of the club is turned down toward the ground and the shaft tilted to the inside or toward the right toe. In this closed position, a hook, a shot which curves to the left, is bound to result.

If the left hand and wrist turn inwardly toward the body, the club is kicked into an open position, which means that the face of the club is turned toward the sky and the club shaft tilted away from the player, away from the right toe. From this position, a slice is produced, and the shot will curve to the right.

Hitting Them Straight. An intermediate position of the club, neither open nor closed, produces a straight-flying shot. However, the only way to learn this desired "happy medium"—a perfectly true or square position—is to learn the two extremes, open and closed, as just explained.

Continuing with Step No. 3, we find that *the pick-up action of the right hand is stopped by the downward thrust of the left hand, and the club can be carried only a short distance from the ball, far enough to form approximately a 45-degree angle.* Now the body pivot takes over to continue the backswing. The pivot draws the right hip back, contracting the right arm and kicking the left knee forward. With no trouble at all, the left arm extends itself, and the top of the swing is reached. In a momentary hesitation at the top of the swing, the knee position is reversed, and the weight shifts to the left leg.

Down and Through

As the knee position is reversed and the weight shifted to the left leg, there is a feeling of the left hip being pulled back, and this actually causes a slight sway of the body in the direction of the shot. When the body is turning into or toward the ball, it is possible to make an almost straight downward pull on the club with the left arm. This generates a centrifugal force which makes the clubhead fly down and into the ball on Step No. 4.

The entire operation could almost be called mechanical. The body winds up on the right leg in the backswing, and then rewinds on the left leg as the club is brought on down and through the ball.

Summary of the Second Four Steps

After getting set in the preliminary four steps, we found that the player should employ the following four steps to carry him through the swing correctly:

STEP NO. 1: This is the first part of the one-two motion of the forward press. The player makes a forward move with the right knee, and the hands swing over past the left knee.

STEP NO. 2: The knee position is reversed, thereby transferring the weight to the right leg. The hands swing back past the ball and are nearly opposite the right knee.

STEP NO. 3: The right hand picks the club up off the ground to start the backswing. The left hand opposes the upward motion, and a downward thrust of the left hand kicks the club into a set position. A body pivot brings the club to the top of the backswing.

STEP NO. 4: The weight shifts to the left leg and the body turns into the ball, causing a downward pull on the club with the left arm, the clubhead travelling down and through the ball.

Looking at the Pictures

Pictures 10–15 portray Step No. 1, the forward press. Photographs 16–21 show the reverse press, Step No. 2, when the weight shifts to the right foot. At this point, Step No. 3 begins, and the next few pictures show the pick-up action of the club by the right hand and arm, and the positioning action of the club by the left hand and arm. Now that the club is cocked, the body pivot movement brings the club to the top of the swing, taking us up through Illustration 30. Pictures 31–45 show the completion of the swing.

THREE

Iron Shots

THE EASY WAY TO PLAY GOLF IS TO LET THE CLUB DO THE WORK. THE procedure used in the playing of an iron shot is the same as that used in playing the woods. The grip, the stance, yes, even the playing of the ball opposite the left foot and the turning out of the right heel all are done in exactly the same way, and the same 1-2-3-4 routine is followed in the swing. Whether wood clubs or iron clubs are being used, all golf shots require the basic operations of footwork, hands, and pivot.

Some Golf Club History

Originally, a golfer who owned four clubs had a complete set. There was the *driver* for the initial long shot, the *brassie,* which got its name from the protective plate of brass attached to the bottom of the club, the *baffy,* a club lofted to raise the ball into the air, and the *putter,* used to roll the ball into the cup.

The curious part about these original clubs is that they were all made of wood, and what is even more noteworthy, they were all constructed of one piece of wood. The handle and the head of the club were one piece of solid hickory, fashioned much like our present-day hockey stick. Later, by joining a hickory handle to another piece of wood which formed the head of the club, the splice type of golf club was constructed.

I once heard of a lady who selected a brassie to play in a one-club tournament. When asked why she selected this particular club, which is rather ill-suited to act as an all-purpose club, she replied that she chose it "because it looks so pretty."

After all-wooden golf clubs had been in use for some time, it was discovered that if an iron blade were used to replace the conventional wooden head of the club, golfers could produce a type of shot which had a tendency to stop where it landed instead of rolling. This was most helpful in approach shots. These iron-bladed clubs originated in Scotland and were called *cleeks.* Various styles of cleeks were introduced—some were used for putting, some for driving, and some for the approach shots.

Number of Clubs Increases. From the original set of four all-wood, all-one-piece clubs, the number of clubs a player used increased to seven, a driver and a brassie for the long drives, and five irons. The irons consisted of a driving cleek for the long iron shots, a lofter or mashie for pitch shots, a niblick for getting out of trouble, a sort of in-between lofted club called a *jigger,* and the putter. There are many golfers who feel that such a limited set of clubs would provide a true test of championship golf if used today.

There were no limitations on the number of clubs a golfer could use in those days, and as the game became more popular in America and the competition became keener, players began to acquire a greater number of clubs. It was not uncommon for a professional golfer to take as many as twenty clubs onto the course. My good friend Harry Cooper, professional at the famous Lakeside Club of Hollywood, employed a bag of twenty-three clubs in one tournament, although some were merely extra drivers and putters. This growing practice of using many clubs was considered as being rather discouraging to anyone planning to take up the game, and finally the United States Golf Association, the body that makes the rules of golf, decreed that a player cannot use more than fourteen clubs in a game.

So, from the original one club of the shepherds, a set of golf clubs became standard at four when only wooden clubs were used, practically rose to infinity when irons were first introduced, and finally levelled off at fourteen when the Golf Association took action. These fourteen clubs are divided into the following categories, which coincide with the three departments of golf shots.

a. The four drivers, which provide a tool for each type of long drive a golfer may be required to play.

b. Nine irons, used for the approach or position shots.

c. The putter, to roll the ball into the cup.

Modern manufacturing methods and development of steel have made it possible to provide clubs that are perfectly balanced sets. They are of very fine workmanship, and available in any desired grade, weight, or style. There is, however, technical consideration with regard to the type of shaft and general balance of golf clubs, and this can have considerable influence on a golfer's game. In this respect, it is best to get qualified advice, particularly from a member of the Professional Golfers Association, who will see that the equipment being used is best suited to the golfer and his purse.

Relative Distances of the Irons. Iron clubs are used solely for the purpose of playing for position, that is, for getting the ball onto the green or, if the player is in trouble, for getting the ball back onto the fairway or in a good position for the next shot.

A complete set of iron clubs, nine altogether, is numbered 1 through 9, the numbers having replaced the individual names previously used for the clubs. The numbers signify the pitch, loft, or angle of each club. The No. 1 iron will drive the ball very low, and consequently send it a great distance, while the No. 9 club will loft the ball sharply, so that it goes up, rather than out away from the player.

The accompanying chart shows the comparative trajectories of the individual irons. A brief study of this chart shows the pattern of relativity that exists between the results obtained from each of the clubs, but the respective results are produced only when all of the clubs are used in exactly the same manner. Each of the irons must be used with the same basic pattern of footwork, which leads to the body pivot, the power-creating operation, which in turn leads to proper hand action, through which the correct directional control is created.

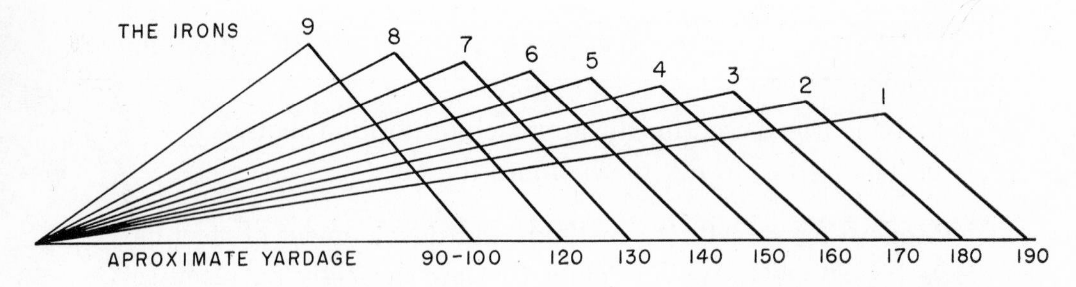

The Footwork and Pivot

In the execution of a golf shot, the footwork and pivot are constant. There is only one way to shift the weight from one foot to the other, and that is by relaxing one knee and straightening the other. For example, relaxing the right knee and straightening the left knee places the weight of the body on the left foot. A reversal of the knee positions places the weight on the right foot.

It is important for every golfer to remember, however, that any

46 47 48

exaggeration of this knee action causes the motion to have just the opposite effect than the one intended. Because they know this and realize the danger of any exaggerated knee action, all good golfers develop and perfect their footwork and knee action to a modified form. Unless a player is schooled in the absolute necessity of doing this operation correctly, he may well be shifting his weight to the wrong foot by exaggerating the motion.

The pivot motion can be done incorrectly, also, if the golfer deviates from the pattern we have described. Once the weight is on the right foot, the only way the player can pivot is by drawing the right hip back, which has the effect of drawing the right arm back, while the left knee is kicked forward. This diagonal motion, with

49 50 51

52 53 54

the left knee and right arm working simultaneously, is the correct motion as the club is taken away from the ball on the backswing, and the reverse criss-cross action involving the left arm and right knee is the correct motion in the downswing. Any other type of motion would destroy the player's sense of balance and create tension, distorting the natural movement of the body and thereby destroying the swing.

Hand Action with the Irons

Although footwork and the pivot are constant, a different situation develops when hand action begins its work in the golf shot.

55 56 57

58 59 60

The hands have the important task of setting or cocking the club at the outset of the backswing. The manner in which the club is positioned at this time becomes the most important part of the golf shot, for it determines the direction in which the ball will travel when it is hit.

Directional hand action is of particular importance in iron shots, because the placement of the ball is of extreme importance when approach shots are being played to a heavily-trapped green, or a certain position is being sought in coming out of the trees or over a bunker or water hazard. This same directional control is needed with the wood clubs, also, but with the woods, the player has the entire fairway to shoot at. With the irons, the goal is only one part of the

61 62 63

64 65 66

green or a certain spot in the fairway. Iron shots call for accuracy, so hand action assumes an added importance with the irons.

When a player finds his ball in difficult spots on the fairway, or in the rough, it sometimes is necessary to play a slice or a hook to get out of the difficulty. This again places a direct responsibility on hand action, because a hook or a slice is produced primarily by cocking the club into an open or closed position.

Types of Iron Shots. The situations a golfer must handle when using the iron clubs are quite varied. There are the regular shots from the fairway to the green, the player relying on each club for its normal performance, and there are shots from uphill, downhill, and

67 68 69

70 71 72

sidehill lies. There may be shots out of deep grass, shots out of the sand, and shots requiring a hook or slice to come out of the trees or around a single tree.

Regardless of the situation, the player is restricted to doing one of three things—playing a normal, straight shot; playing a slice, the shot that curves to the right; or playing a hook, the shot that curves to the left. Shots that climb very high in their flight all have a tendency to flare or drift to the right. These shots stop quickly on landing—they are the slices. Then there are the shots that fly very low in trajectory. They are contrary to a slice and all have a tendency

73 74 75

76 77 78

to curve to the left and roll after landing on the ground—they are the hooks. An in-between shot, with neither a curve to the right nor to the left, is the perfect shot in direction, flight, and effect. This is the straight shot.

Golfers are confronted with many situations during a game, and the shot they make in any given situation will depend upon the effect that is desired and the position in which the ball is lying. Playing for position emphasizes again the need for the player to have a good basic understanding of hand action.

Gripping the Irons. Contrary to a common impression, it is not

79 80 81

82 83 84

necessary to grip the iron clubs any tighter than the woods. Some golfers seem to have the idea that, because many iron shots are played from cuppy lies or from deep grass and the club does come in contact with the ground, iron shots require a tighter grip. Nothing could be more harmful, because a tense grip destroys the correct hand action necessary to get the club into the proper position to produce the desired effect.

To refute the idea that a player needs a tight grip for the irons, let me give you an illustration. When an expert swings a driver, the head of the club at the time it meets the ball is travelling at a speed of from 1,000 to 1,200 feet a second. With the irons, the clubhead may not be moving that fast, but it is still travelling at high speed. With the driver, the clubhead travels at the rate of 600 to 700 miles an hour at the moment of impact. Considering that the head of a golf club weighs from 8 to 10 ounces, we have the situation of a half a pound traveling at 600 miles per hour. It can be seen that the weight of the clubhead in motion is a weight that the fingers can do very little about. Is it any wonder that beginners, fighting the natural movement of the club, get blisters so easily? One of our great professional stars recently caused an injury to his left hand because he had too tight a grip.

85 86 87

If the weight is shifted correctly and the body pivot and hand action have been fitted together properly in the backswing, the downswing is easy and natural. What happens on the way up determines how the club will come through, for things move so fast in the downswing, and such a powerful force has been set in motion, that the golfer can do little to change the result once the downswing has begun. Therefore, a golfer who concentrates on perfecting the upswing, or backswing, will be well along the road to better golf. There can be little variation in the footwork and body pivot of a golf shot, but there can be deliberate variations with the hands to position the club, and this is most important of all, because it determines where the ball will fly.

Importance of the Waggle. Realizing that hand action is so important in a shot, good golfers do considerable waggling of the club before they begin the backswing. Many onlookers consider these preliminary motions as being attributable to nervousness, temperament, or a general effort to relax, but such is not the case. These experienced players are merely getting the feel of the club, so their hand action in the shot will be as nearly flawless as possible.

88 89 90

Movies of the Golf Shot

Many motion pictures have been taken of a golf swing, and invariably the preliminary pictures are discarded and only those parts of the film showing the upswing and the downswing are retained. This is most unfortunate, because the finished reel does not portray the initial footwork or weightshift which enables the player to properly prepare himself for the actual swing. Neither does it show the all-important hand action or the early wrist-break with which the player determines the type of shot to be made. It is also impossible to see how the player uses his hands to cock or position the club for the shot.

In a similar manner, the author, in his early efforts to work out a plan or method of teaching golf, became elated at having developed a way of explaining the mechanics of the necessary footwork, the relationship of this footwork to the body pivot, and the importance of the pivot as the actual means of swinging the club. After continued trials and tests, I enthusiastically did a series of radio lectures, transcribed these into a set of magazine articles, and eventually helped to produce a motion picture reel on the subject.

91 92 93

Repeated study of these films, more tests on the golf course, and more trick shot exhibitions revealed that there was no reference to the cocking of the club by the hands in those films and articles. This part of a golf swing is not an easy thing to discern, because at the outset of the backswing the action of the hands in cocking the club and the action of the body pivot actually occur simultaneously. No camera or series of pictures can portray what can be referred to as a kind of sleight of hand performance, unless the relationship and synchronization of the two actions are specifically brought to the viewer's attention. It all becomes quite simple when one understands it, but until it is taken apart and thoroughly examined, this phase of golf can continue to be an elusive and noncomprehensible matter.

George Jacobus, former president of the Professional Golfers Association and for years the instructor at the Ridgewood Country Club in New Jersey, made a concerted effort to get better motion pictures of the golf swing to help golfers get a better understanding of its intricacies. Always a diligent worker for the advancement of golf, Jacobus was very much interested in furthering studies of golf and golf instruction. During his term of office, a fund was made available to secure a motion picture camera that took 3200 exposures per second. Previous cameras could only get 16 exposures per second, so the new device appeared to be the means of getting all the innermost secrets of a golf swing on film.

After taking pictures of Bobby Jones in this country, the machine and its operators were sent to England to get pictures of Harry Vardon and the dean of all women golfers at that time, Joyce Wethered.

The final result was disappointing, for the pictures failed to do the expected. The golf shot was depicted on the screen about 100 times slower than normal, and practically all of the preliminary motion was cut off because the film was extremely long. Also, it was found that no motion picture, no matter how fast or slow, can separate hand action from body action, unless the player definitely sets out to portray that one phase particularly.

Despite the fact that the film failed to do all that was expected of it, Jacobus and the PGA are to be complimented for their solicitous expenditure of time and money in their efforts to give golfers a better understanding of the game.

Getting Set for the Swing

If a player studies professional golfers in action, he will notice that before they begin their swing, they actually make a false start with the club, using the wiggle-waggle action. These experienced golfers go into the one-two of the swing, the forward press and a reverse press, but instead of taking off into the backswing they make a distinctive flip of the clubhead toward the right toe and then return the club to the ball. They repeat this same procedure once more, returning the club to the ball, go through the one-two motion again, and then before you know it the club is up, down, and through the swing.

It should be remembered that the amount of pivot regulates the power of the shot. The two sets of pictures in this chapter show both the long- and short-iron swings. For longer distance, an increased turn of the body or a full turn would produce a long shot, and a lesser turn, a quarter turn, for example, would produce a shorter shot.

94. If the ball is resting in a hollow, or for some other reason has a bad lie, it is played much nearer the right foot, as shown in the picture at the left. *(See pages 70 and 72.)*

Hooking and Slicing

To slice or curve a shot to the right, a player must set or cock his club in an open position at the outset of the backswing, and he must keep the entire swing in this slice groove to get the desired result. If a golfer wants to produce a hook or curve the ball to the left, the club position must be reversed and the club cocked in a closed position and maintained that way throughout the swing. Obviously, if the open position produces a slice and the closed position a hook, the neutral or square position will produce a straight-flying shot. "The angle of reflection is equal to the angle of incidence" is an old, positive, and unwavering principle which applies to a golf shot the same as it does to anything else.

Open and Closed Club Positions. To set the club in an open position for a slice, the player merely turns his left hand and left wrist in toward the body as the club is started on the backswing by the right hand. This will turn the face of the club toward the sky and tilt the shaft away from the right foot so that the club will swing out from the player on the backswing and across the line of the shot from the outside as the ball is met.

For a closed position, the player must turn the left hand and wrist out and away from the body as the club is started on the backswing by the right hand. This outward movement turns the face of the club toward the ground and tilts the shaft of the club to the inside of the line of the shot, toward the right toe. In this position, the club swings from the inside to the outside as the ball is being met.

The Stance for the Hook and Slice. Many golfers have the idea that a hook or slice is entirely the result of stance or foot position. This is not true, for stance plays only a secondary or contributory role in this phase of golf. Assuming an open stance will place the body in a position that will facilitate making a slice shot, and therefore it should be used when playing a slice. The open stance is one in which the right foot is advanced to a point nearer the line of the shot. In this advanced position, the body is angled so that the shoulders are pointed to the left of the line of the shot, and such a position causes the club to be carried back and forth on that angle. Consequently, it meets the ball from the outside and causes it to turn and twist off to the right in its flight.

The reverse position of the right foot should be used when playing for a hook. That is, the right foot should be drawn back from the line parallel to the line of the shot, and this places the body so that the shoulders are pointed to the right of the line of the shot. This foot position aids the golfer in swinging the club back on the inside and down toward the outside, tending to spin the ball so it curves to the left.

Effects of the Slice and the Hook. In a hook shot, the ball has a great deal of overspin. That is, it is turning in the direction it is moving or travelling. This tends to keep the flight of the ball low, and it also veers it off to the left. Because of the overspin, the ball rolls after it lands in a hook shot, and in playing these shots to the green, allowance must be made for this roll. Such a shot is called a *pitch-and-run* shot. With their low flight and ultimate roll, these shots are advantageous when the golfer is playing into a strong wind.

The slice, on the other hand, acts in the reverse manner. It has an emphatic backspin on it, making it spin backwards toward the player as it travels away from him. This backspin causes the shot to climb high into the air and tend to drift off to the right. Such a shot stops quickly when it lands, sometimes almost jumping backward when it hits if there is enough backspin on it. This is called a *pitch* shot, the opposite of the pitch-and-run shot just described.

At one time it was insisted that the only way to play an iron shot to the green and make the ball stop when it landed there was to use this left-to-right shot or slice. However, modern, well-groomed golf greens with the proper degree of moisture and softness in the turf, permit the use of a right-to-left shot with equally good results.

No matter what type of shot is being made, including a hook or slice, the weight shift and body action remain the same in almost every case. The weight is on the right foot for the backswing and on the left foot for the downswing. The weight should be on the left foot as the ball is being hit. Whether the shot hooks, slices, or goes straight depends upon how the club was cocked by the hands. Of course, there may be an open stance with the feet to facilitate a body pivot more conducive to slicing, or a closed stance to get a body turn helpful to hooking. But the player should remember that the basic cause of a hook or slice is the positioning or cocking of the

95 (left) and 96 (below). If the ball lies in deep grass, foot, hand, and body positions are the same as in a normal shot but the ball is played at a point more opposite the right heel. The club is therefore tilted forward and down on the ball. The picture below shows the top of the swing. Note that the hands have kept the club in a position "square with the ball," and that the left arm is natural, straight, and without tension.

97 (right). Just after the impact with the ball in deep grass. The club automatically digs down into the grass and brings the ball out.

club through the hand action. The body action is but a secondary cause.

It can be seen that, because the player's weight is on the left foot when the ball is being hit, even in a hook or slice, the ball should always be played opposite the left foot. The right foot may be moved forward or backward from the line parallel to the line of the shot, but the ball must be lined up opposite the left foot every time, for the weight is off the right foot when the ball is being hit. The left foot is the important one at the time of impact.

Importance of Weight Shift. The author is not discounting the importance of proper weight shift in a golf shot. Improper weight shift can cause a distorted pivot, which makes the proper positioning of the club by the hands impossible. This shows once again the need of an orderly sequence in a golf shot, with the correct footwork and body turn as one phase, and the accompanying hand action as another phase. There must be proper coordination and synchronization of these two operations, one of which provides the power of the shot and the other the direction.

Playing the Lies and Trouble Shots

In golf, as in everything else, there are exceptions to the rule, and there are several exceptions to the rule of playing the ball opposite the left foot. When the ball sets in a depression or a cuppy lie, or when it lies in the sand or the deep grass, we have a situation where the ball is really below the level of the shot. It is below the level on which the player is standing. If such a shot were played with the ball opposite the left foot, the player would meet the ball above center and top it or drive it down into the ground.

Any time the ball is lower than the level of the player's feet, the club must be placed in an off-center position on Step No. 1 of the first four steps. When placing the club to the ball with the left hand, the player should tilt it or turn it over on the ball as if he were going to drive the ball into the ground. Placing the club to the ball in this manner automatically produces a position in which the ball is

98 (left). This picture shows how the ball should be played out of a sand trap on a short, 40-yard shot. The ball is shown here in relation to the normal club position.

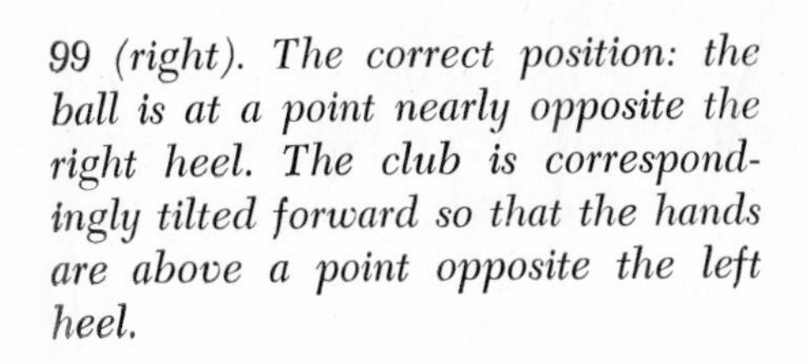

99 (right). The correct position: the ball is at a point nearly opposite the right heel. The club is correspondingly tilted forward so that the hands are above a point opposite the left heel.

opposite a point equal with the center of the body. In some extreme cases, the ball is at a point opposite the right foot instead of the left foot. From such a position, an automatic effect of having the clubhead swing down and into the turf is produced. When the ball is in the sand, the grass, or a cuppy lie, such an effect must be produced or the shot just will not get away.

Naturally, the further back one has to play the ball (when not playing it opposite the left foot), the more lofted club he must use. This situation often gives rise to the idea that a golfer should play a No. 4 iron from one spot, a No. 6 iron from another, a No. 8 from another, and so on. However, this is the case only when playing the exception, as when playing from lies, sand, or tall grass. It is *not* the case when playing normal shots.

Trouble Shooting. Trouble shots, such as those from bad lies, deep grass, sand, or depressions, all are played by gradually shifting the position of the ball from a point directly opposite the left heel to a point more nearly opposite the right foot. How far back the player should play the ball depends upon the gravity of the situation. The worse the situation is, or the steeper the lie, the farther back the ball should be played and the more lofted the club.

Sidehill Lies. Sidehill lies really fall into the category of hooks and slices. Whenever the player is standing in a position where the ball is below the level of his feet, then a natural slice will be produced. The logical solution is to purposely allow for the slice, but if conditions prevent that, the player must counteract the slice by closing the club to secure a straight-flying shot.

When the player finds himself in the opposite position, when he has to stand lower than the spot at which the ball rests, a hook will be the natural result if he employs his usual swing. If it is impractical to play for the hook, the player must allow for this situation by opening the club to get a straight-flying shot.

In any sidehill situation, it is best not to overswing. The golfer should not try for too long a shot, for he may lose his footing or balance and ruin the shot. It is better to use a stronger club, play a

100 (left) and 101 (below). At left I am shown at the top of my swing in a sand trap, and below just before impact with the ball. Note that although the ball is not in normal position, there are evident the usual features of the swing: weight on right foot, straight left arm, and club square with line of shot.

102 (right). Here you see the finish of a 40-yard trap shot swing. Note how sand was contacted when the shot was played.

shorter swing, and keep the stance narrow to maintain balance more easily.

Downhill and Uphill Lies. The downhill lie, where the ground falls away in the direction of the shot, most likely will produce a slice, and the uphill lie, where the ground rises abruptly in the direction of the shot, usually results in a hook. The rules just cited should be kept in mind when playing these lies, and the player will find it helpful in both cases to play the ball back off the right foot more. In both downhill and uphill lies, this trouble-shot stance gives more solid contact with the ball, thereby producing a better shot.

Sand Shots. Sand makes a difficult hazard to play on any golf course. When the ball gets into it, it often is buried or lying in a depression. On the Oakmont course in Pittsburgh, a special rake was devised to make furrows about three inches apart in the sand hazards, and the ball always manages to get half buried in one of these furrows. When playing out of sand, the golfer should follow this plan: Size up the lie to determine how deep the ball is lying. This will show how much sand must be removed to get to the bottom of the ball with the swing of the club. Avoid "taking sand" if you possibly can, for the sand is the uncertain or treacherous part of the shot.

After deciding about the lie and the amount of sand to be taken, make up your mind what type of shot you have to play. If you must raise the ball sharply and stop it suddenly, open the club and play a slice or a cut shot. This is not an easy shot, so if you possibly can avoid it you should do so, using the reverse shot, closing the clubface and standing with the ball opposite the right foot. With this closed-face shot, it is possible to have the club descend sharply on the ball and meet it before encountering the sand. This gets the ball away cleanly in many cases, producing a shot with a pitch-and-run effect, low in flight, but sufficient to get the ball out of most traps.

In the execution of sand shots, the usual procedure of weight shift, cocking of the club, and body pivot are followed, but the important thing is to determine beforehand whether the cut shot is necessary or whether the ordinary pitch-and-run shot will get the ball away. The use of the heavy sand-iron type of club is highly recommended. This club works equally well in high grass when you use the same procedure outlined for the sand shots.

Some Concluding Iron Shots

A common golf expression says that all good golfers "hit against a straight left leg." Personally, I do not like this adage, because it can be misleading. It is sufficient for the player to remember that for a good golf swing he must have the weight on the right foot in the backswing and on the left foot in the downswing and follow-through.

So powerful was the body motion of Bobby Jones as he went "through" the ball that not only did his right heel leave the ground, but the turn on his left leg was so great and the pulling back of his left hip and side so strong that his left leg was turned to a point where it actually raised up the left heel from the inside of his left foot.

A more recent star, Cary Middlecoff, is an unusually long hitter, his excellent footwork being a big factor in enabling him to pull down and through the ball with a terrific leftside action. Middlecoff is so decidedly on his left foot when the club hits the ball that the entire inside part of his left foot is off the ground at this point.

As further support of this discussion about having the weight on the left foot at the time of impact, consider the words of Sam Snead when he was asked to explain what he thought of when making a shot. Snead described the situation rather thoroughly in this terse statement: "I always make sure that I do a forward press, and then I make certain that I get back to my left foot before the club hits the ball."

Using the Right Club. Buying a set of irons is a waste of money unless the player learns to swing each of the clubs in exactly the same way. Only then will each club have a purpose and effect of its own and be of real value to the player. On any normal shot, the

103 (left). Here is the top of the swing in a sand trap slice shot. Note that my right foot is in an advanced position and that the ball is played at a point forward or opposite the left toe. 104 (right) shows the swing just after impact with the ball.

golfer merely lets the club produce the shot for which it was designed, employing his usual swing and letting the club do the work.

If for some reason it is necessary to make the ball stop when it lands, the club must be swung in an open position. This produces backspin and a certain amount of sidespin. The backspin causes a natural loss of distance, and the sidespin gives the shot a slice or curve to the right. When playing such a shot, the player must take into consideration the loss of distance and allow for the change in the direction of flight. It may be necessary to use a stronger club for this shot, for example, a No. 7 iron instead of a No. 9, or a No. 3 iron rather than a No. 5.

For a little extra distance, or when he wants the ball to roll after landing or is playing into the wind, the player can purposely play for a hook. This is done by cocking the club in a closed position, which causes the ball to travel low and curve to the left.

By maneuvering the club from an open to a closed position and back again, the golfer gets a good sense of the correct club position for each individual shot. This calls for a fine sense of hand action, without the slightest trace of tenseness or tightness in the grip.

Picturing the Swing

The pictures accompanying this chapter on iron shots portray the procedure described here. The first group shows the swing with a long iron; the second group shows a short-iron swing.

Illustration 46 is the address at the ball. Illustration 47 shows the forward press, Step No. 1. The reverse press, Step No. 2, is pictured in Illustration 48.

The part of the swing in which the right hand and arm are picking the club up off the ground is shown in Illustrations 49–52. Illustrations 53–54 portray the downward thrust of the left hand.

The pivot begins in Illustration 55. Illustrations 51–61 picture the upswing or backswing, carried out through the pivot. As the right arm is drawn back, the left arm tends to extend itself and aid in keeping the club in the position in which it has been set.

Illustrations 62–65 picture the downswing. Here, the knees reverse their position and the weight is shifted to the left foot. With a reverse pivot of the body, the left arm pulls the club right down on the ball. Impact is shown in Illustration 66, and from there on we see the natural follow-through in Illustrations 67–72.

Illustrations 73–93 show the swing with a short iron.

FOUR

Putting

"A good putter is a match for any golfer."
"We drive for show but we putt for dough."

THESE TWO MAXIMS EXPRESS THE IMPORTANCE ALL GOOD GOLFERS place on the putting phase of the game. A study of the three departments of golf—driving, approaching, and putting—reveals that from forty to fifty per cent of the strokes are used up on the putting green. A par golfer whose scores average around 72 makes approximately thirty to thirty-eight putts per round. A player who scores in the 80's uses from thirty-four to forty putts each round, and one who cards near 100 takes from thirty-six to fifty shots on the putting green each time around.

Bobby Jones, the "Grand Slam" champion, felt he was putting

badly if he took more than thirty putts for the eighteen holes. Today, golf competition is very keen, and our professional stars are so evenly matched on the drives and approaches that victory generally goes to the player who is "dropping his putts."

Always known as a mediocre putter, Sam Snead hit a hot streak on the greens back in 1950 and gave much credit to a center-shafted blade style putter. Fred Daly, who won the British Open in 1947, credits much of his low scoring to a hickory-shafted putter he picked up on a South African tour. Many of the below-par scores by the great professionals are attributed to "hot putters."

Important as putting is in golf, it has been presented by many as something that cannot be taught. There has been an idea among golfers that good putters are born and not made, and that the magic touch on the putting greens is a gift of the gods that humans cannot cultivate.

It Can Be Taught

Putting can be taught and learned very easily. The requirements of putting are no different than the requirements of any other shot in golf. In putting, the golfer must be able to hit the ball straight, and that means *direction.* He also must be able to gauge the length of the putt, and that means *distance.* It is in the matter of distance that most golfers err on the putting green. The average golfer lacks the ability to estimate the speed or distance of his putts, and this difficulty causes much trouble on the short approaches.

It usually goes something like this. Confronted with a 25- or 30-foot putt, the player, lacking the confidence he should have, cautiously strokes the ball and very often finds it coming to a stop 10 or 12 feet short of the cup. Concluding that this particular green must be "slow," he charges into his next putt, overshooting the mark by five or six feet. The next putt probably misses too, so the player has poured four strokes down the drain. This is easy to do if the golfer does not have the proper control or sense of distance on the green.

Pulling to the Left. Statistics show that 80 per cent of the short putts that miss the cup do so because *they are pulled off the line to the left.* On putts from three to ten feet, there is a definite inability to keep the ball on the line and a decided lack of directional control. This situation generally plagues the low handicap golfer as well as the high handicap man. There are countless stories of how titles and championships have been lost on short putts.

At the time Cary Middlecoff was endeavoring to win his first PGA championship, he got through the dreaded 18-hole matches and was on his way, with one up and one to go in his 36-hole quarter-final match against Ted Kroll. Things looked better when Middlecoff played a perfect tee shot and Kroll's tee effort went into the woods. Kroll had to play a sacrifice shot, and he finally came onto the green within 10 feet of the cup, using three shots.

Meanwhile, playing it safe, Middlecoff put his second shot just short of the green about 70 feet from the pin. His third shot carried the ball to within five feet of the cup. Middlecoff could win the match by getting a tie on this last hole. At this point, Kroll sank his 10-foot putt for a four. Middlecoff pulled his five-foot putt off to the left of the cup to lose the hole, and subsequently the match on the second extra hole.

The Search for the Secret. Because of these three things—the idea that putting cannot be taught, the difficulty in gauging distance, and the tendency to pull the short putts off the line—golfers continually buy new putters, change their stance, change their grip, and experiment. They do everything but getting right down to some real practice, which is the only thing that will give them the proper sense of direction and feel in putting.

It is impossible to know how many different types and models of putters have been designed in the hope of finding something that will drop the ball into the cup consistently. My friend Fred X. Fry, golf professional at Pacific Grove, California, has accumulated 136 different kinds of putters.

However, the answer cannot be found in the type of putter used. It is contained within the player himself, for after all, the club will do only what he makes it do. A golfer who is a good putter gets good results with any type or design of putter. However, I draw the line when it comes to the newly-introduced croquet style putter, which I feel belongs in the game of croquet and not in golf.

The simple, easy way to learn to putt is to follow the same rules that produce the desired results in the other shots in golf. In driving the ball, a golfer must have distance and direction in approaching, he needs an even finer degree of the same two elements; in putting, distance and direction must be near-perfect. For this reason, it can be seen that, if a certain pattern or form is necessary to produce the desired results in driving and approaching, the same requirements should give good results in putting. A procedure which provides directional and distance control on shots from 100 to 250 yards should prove to be bullseye perfect at 5, 10, or 20 feet.

The Pivot

A study of the form prescribed for driving reveals that it was body pivot which actually made the club swing, determining the intensity of the swing or just how much power was being applied to the club. The same holds true for putting. In the body pivot, players develop a system of *quartering* their swing, a means of gauging the power applied to the club. For example, a full body pivot will drive a golf ball 200 yards easily. To drive the ball about one-half that distance, the player makes only a half pivot. A quarter of

105 *106* *107*

108 *109* *110*

a pivot would produce only a quarter of the power, driving the ball approximately 50 yards.

This business of quartering the swing, that is, playing a three-quarter, half, or quarter swing, has been called antiquated, because of the modern sets of matched irons and woods in use today. This is not true. The only way to learn to gauge the force in a golf swing is through the quartering technique. Because of the varying distances required in approach shots, quartering is absolutely necessary in playing short iron shots to the green, but this technique is equally applicable to wood shots through the fairway.

This same formula of the body pivot, when used in putting, not only gives a sense of basic accuracy but also provides the feel of distance by regulating the amount of swing of the club. When applied and established, the resulting putting stroke will be found to be a gem of consistency with relation to distance, and it will prove delightfully easy and surprisingly efficient with regard to accuracy. Three-putting and four-putting of the greens will disappear almost immediately if this body pivot type of putting stroke is adopted. With very little practice, a player can develop a natural, coordinated movement, enabling him to consistently lay the ball within inches of the cup from 30-foot, yes, even 40-foot, distances.

111 *112* *113*

Hand Action in the Pivot. In putting, as in all other golf shots, directional control is the result of hand action. In addition to the basic swinging control from the body, there must be direction from the hands. This is developed by employing the hands in the same manner as in the drives and iron shots. The hands have the job of setting or cocking the putter in the proper position to produce proper directional control over the shot.

Make a Motion

Objections may arise to the plan as we have outlined it, describing it as too complicated. However, the procedure actually is most simple. What could be more natural than having your body and hands working together harmoniously to produce the shot? What could be more impractical and confusing than to have a conflict of motion between hands and body? How annoying this can be when executing the one movement in golf requiring the special delicacy of action that the fine sense of a putting touch requires.

Only through perfect rhythm and coordination of body and hand movement can this putting touch, the dream of all golfers, be acquired. To make golf enjoyable, to make it fun, the player should develop this phase of the game, for it's no fun to make a 250-yard drive and a nice approach shot to within six feet of the cup, only to spoil it all by missing the six-foot putt. Simplicity in putting is not the result of eliminating certain factors of the basic operation. On the contrary, it is the result of combining the necessary movements into one coordinated whole.

Added to the idea that putting is something which only a few lucky golfers inherit, there are objections by some players to swaying and to even the slightest movement of the head. What have become broad and general objections in the regular shots have become strict, rigid, and emphatic objections in the putting stroke. This belief that there should be absolute tenseness and rigidity of body position while putting has been the cause of many short putts being pulled off the line to the left, as we have illustrated. If there were no other reason to object, I feel that this alone is sufficient ground for disputing this mistaken theory. For the sake of grace, naturalness, ease, and effectiveness, there is no substitute for a bodily-controlled putting stroke.

Putting Styles of Jones and Diegel. Bobby Jones and Leo Diegel were two outstanding golfers who advocated body control in putting. Jones, with his quota of thirty putts for eighteen holes, gave this advice: "When putting," he said, "be sure to assume a comfortable, relaxed position to the ball—then sweep the putter back in a low swing motion, and if the body has a tendency to move with

114 115 116

117 *118* *119*

the motion, let it do so." This confirms the great golf star's belief that there should be body motion in putting, but I would go him one further and advise golfers to learn to regulate the swing of the putter with body motion.

Diegel, former PGA and Canadian champion, had much difficulty with his putting at one time. In fact, it became almost tragic. He was employed by George McLean as a private golf instructor and playing companion, and McLean was inclined to depend upon Diegel's game rather than his own. With close matchmaking, the result invariably depended upon sinking those four-foot and five-foot putts,

120 *121* *122*

and Leo began to find the responsibility quite burdensome. In an effort to work out a foolproof stroke, he began copying the style of every successful putter he saw.

Diegel found that one golfer who seemed to putt very well kept his right elbow firmly against his body as he putted. A short time later he met a golfer who kept his left elbow firmly against his side as he swung. Diegel tried first one style, then the other, and finally decided to keep both elbows against the body during the swing. This was the beginning of the Leo Diegel pendulum putting stroke, which is actually nothing more than tieing up the arms in such a way as to make it impossible to swing the club any other way than with the body. Diegel did some mighty fine putting with this stroke, a method termed by many as unorthodox.

As Bobby Jones suggested, and as Leo Diegel found out through trial and error, there is no substitute for a free, easy body motion when you have to "rap that ball into the back of the cup," as the golfing expression goes.

Grip and Stance for Putting

The same general pattern is used in getting ready for the putting stroke as was employed for the drives and iron shots. Step No. 1 is to place the club behind the ball with the left hand. Getting the feet properly placed is the object of Step No. 2. Place the left foot

123

124

125

so that a line from the ball to the left heel will be at a right angle to the line of the putt, the ball being at a point opposite the left heel. The right foot is placed so that the toes are on a line parallel to the line of the putt, although the player may find it advantageous to advance the right foot somewhat to develop a feeling of facing the hole slightly and being a little behind the ball. This is not too important. By all means, however, keep the feet close together. In fact, it would not be amiss to have the heels so close together that they actually touch each other.

In Step No. 3, relax the right knee so that the right hand can be brought to the club. When this is done, instead of overlapping with only the little finger of the right hand, overlap with two fingers. When putting, curl the little finger of the left hand so that the end of it goes under the club shaft rather than around it, actually keeping this finger off the putter handle. This grip concentrates the club control in the forepart of each hand. It practically eliminates pronation of the clubhead, tending to keep the surface of the head square with the line at all times.

Turn the right heel out slightly on Step No. 4, just as in all other shots. This gives us the completed position, and we are ready for the swing.

The Putting Stroke

The position the player finds himself in at the conclusion of the first four steps is identical with the position he will be in at the time the clubhead is striking the ball. Analyzing this position, the golfer finds that he is balanced on his left foot with the ball opposite the left heel. His right knee is slightly relaxed, and the club is being held very lightly with the forepart of each hand.

With the weight on the left foot, the player is restrained from swinging the club unless he shifts the weight to the right foot. To do this, he makes a prompting move with the right knee, a slight forward motion, thereby swinging the hands forward slightly. This is Step No. 1 of the swing, a combination of knee and hand movement called the *forward press.* Step No. 2 is the reverse press, with the knees reversing position so that the weight is shifted to the right foot and the hands swung back to a point nearly opposite the right knee.

Of course, all the movements in putting are very modified and limited. They must be, for the club is swung so very lightly and the ball struck so gently that the putting stroke is called a putting "touch." This is necessary because of the extreme delicacy of swing needed on many of the very "fast" putting surfaces. The putting movements are on a minute scale, and so delicate that they are hardly discernible if not thoroughly understood.

With the weight on the right foot and the hands nearly opposite the right knee, or at least more so than in the previous step, we find that the weight of the club handle is in the right hand. Step No. 3 begins at this point with an upward lift of the club by the right hand. As this is being done, a countering action by the left hand pushes down on the club handle. Just as in all other golf shots, the left hand, depending upon whether it turns toward the body or away from it, cocks the club into an open or a closed position. If either one of these extremes occurs, the ball will be pushed off to the right or to the left, as the case may be. The hands must coordinate to place the club in the desired position, so that the ball will roll straight. A slight backward pull of the right hip produces the body pivot to swing the club away from the ball, and Step No. 3 is completed.

Step No. 4 is a backward pull of the left hip and a reverse pivot of the body, carrying the club through in a perfect pendulum style.

Avoiding the Pitfalls. At first, there is bound to be exaggeration and overemphasis in the putting stroke, causing the player to hit the ball too hard and roll it too far. However, continued repetition of the form presented will enable him to tone down the movements to the degree necessary for perfect results.

A study of the cocking motion should soon develop the ability to determine the position of the clubhead. Conscious guidance of the clubhead in this manner will give the feel of the swing, so the player will know when the clubhead is in line to roll the ball straight.

126. Here is the front view of the left-hand grip for putting. The left thumb is in the normal position on the shaft, the V is pointing to my right shoulder, and the club is in the normal position, as is the ball. The feet are closer together, and the heels are close enough so that no extreme knee action is required.

127. The underside view of the left-hand grip shows how the little finger is curled under the shaft. The left hand grip is normal in every respect but this. Placing the little finger in this position prevents a tense or tight grip.

128. (right). Here is the right-hand putting position. Notice the overlap of the two fingers to prevent tension. 129 (right, below) shows the completed putting grip. With the exceptions noted in pictures 127 and 128, the hands are in the same general position as for all shots. 130 (below, left) illustrates the start of the backswing. The club has been swung back with a delicate, almost imperceptible motion of the body. Here the hands have kept the club as it was at the outset of the swing, and the body turn is giving a true pendulum swing to the stroke.

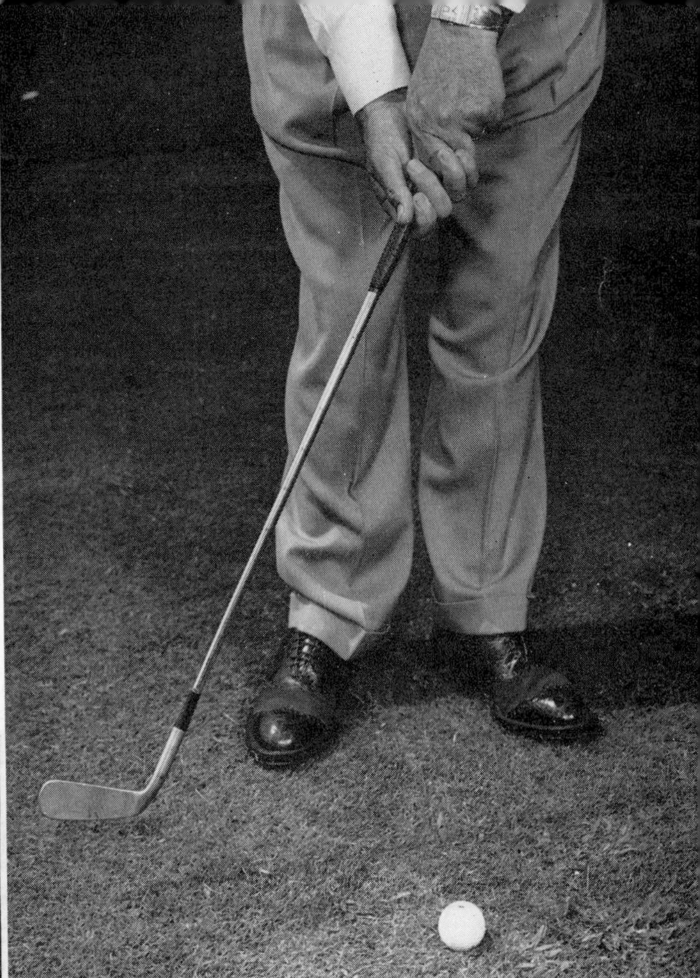

Once this feel of clubhead position is developed, only the intensity of body pivot must be added to get proper swing force.

Remember that there is no short cut in putting, just as there is no short cut in any other golf shot. The first series of four steps will soon develop into an automatic method of getting up to the ball and aiming the shot in a free, comfortable manner. Once this position is attained, the second set of four steps will enable the player to execute the perfect putting stroke, rolling the ball straight and true, and with the right amount of force behind it. Conscientious adherence to these steps will produce the desired distance and direction so important on those keen, fast putting surfaces.

I recognize the fact that there are more ways than one to skin a cat, and, as evidenced by the numerous putter models previously mentioned, there are more ways than one to swing a putter. This is because there is no great amount of force or power needed in the operation. A great number of golfers, because they are never able to (or refuse to learn how to) coordinate the workings of both hands, eventually solve the problem by putting with one hand. To me, this is an admission of weakness, and it is apt to prove costly, because such a procedure can cause havoc with the short shots just off the green, the chip shots.

Shanking and Missed Putts. How often golfers shank chip shots or pull their short putts off to the left of the cup! It's all because of a lack of body pivot. When there is a lack of pivot, there is bound to be a twisting, distorting action throughout the hands, wrists, and forearms, resulting in an unstable, uncertain, and erratic club position, and when this happens, it is impossible to have any directional control.

In the motion picture "Follow The Sun," a story based on the life of Ben Hogan, viewers had a good opportunity to study Hogan's putting style. The pictures reveal that when Hogan addresses the ball he assumes a position equivalent to that we have recommended as taking place at the end of Step No. 2. His left knee is relaxed, and his right knee is fairly straight. In other words, Hogan eliminates Steps Nos. 1 and 2, the forward press and reverse press, starting right in with Step No. 3.

Some Putting Tips

Be sure to stick to the form completely—*no short cuts.*

Always keep the feet close together. This makes weight shifting easier, and comfortable foot position gives a free and relaxed feeling throughout the body. Keeping both knees slightly bent, as in a semi-sitting position, is helpful in putting as well as in chip shots. This relaxed knee position gives balance, poise, and ease of body motion.

Concentrate the grip in the forepart of each hand. This will eliminate tension. Use the double overlap on the right hand and the underlap of the little finger of the left hand to get this grip concentration automatically.

Always make a comparatively full but rather slow swing of the club. This gives a natural follow-through movement to the stroke. Some golfers who are good putters use a formula of one inch of swing for each foot the putt must travel. Of course, this varies, depending upon the texture of the turf.

Some players find it helpful to think of the ball as a wheel, the putter being used as a means to roll the wheel into the cup.

On long putts, it is wise to visualize a three-foot circle around the cup, for the purpose of rolling the first putt into the immediate cup area. If a putt breaks to the right or the left, remember that the ball will travel straight for the first part of the putt and then gradually drift off on its own momentum on the *break* or slope. Learn to decide at what point the ball will start to break, aim for that point, and let the ball float on in from there. The breaking point naturally will be late in an uphill putt and early in a downhill putt.

Grain on the Green. When the green has considerable grain, a putt going against the grain must be harder hit than one going with the grain. The grain is against the player if the blades of the grass lean toward him, and with the player if they lean away from him.

Only certain types of grass develop grain, these being the Bermuda and bent varieties, which spread by sending out shoots or runners. Such spreading produces the grain tendency, causing the blades of grass all to lean in one direction. Generally, if the grain is against the player, the grass has a darker color, because dark shadows appear between the blades.

Some days, all of the putts will drop. On others, none seem to want to go into the cup. This is due, of course, to unseen breaks or rolls in the green or turf. A well-hit putt, however, has a steady forward roll on the ball, and it automatically climbs or rolls over these unseen irregularities more evenly. A putt of this type also is easier to gauge, because it travels over the top of whatever obstacles it encounters, rather than bumping directly against them.

"Never Up, Never In." This has been a slogan in golf for a long time, and it means that golfers should shoot past the hole in the hope of having the ball drop before finishing its roll. Personally, however, I like the theory Bobby Jones had about putting. He said, "If I shoot my putt hard, I have only one side of the cup to go in, the back of the cup. But if I lag my putts to the cup, I have three sides that the ball may go in, the front, both sides, and sometimes even the back."

Putter Types. The ordinary plain-blade putter is still a very efficient tool. Blade putters are exceptionally good on very fast greens, and the mallet-head type, along with the aluminum-head models, is preferred on the heavier turf greens. The latter type is very popular, because it has a broad base which automatically keeps the club steady as it is placed behind the ball. This type naturally rests steadily and gives an air of confidence that the club is "headed right" at the start.

Many golfers are constantly seeking putters with a very upright lie, that is, a club on which the handle comes up very sharp. This type of putter is sought because it presumably will tend to produce a pendulum-type swing. I do not subscribe to this belief, and I definitely recommend a flat-lie putter. As I see it, the flat-lie putter gives the player a better perspective of the ball, the line of the putt, and the cup itself. It is much easier to oversee the situation if the ball is slightly away from the player instead of underneath his chin, or right next to his toes, a position which requires the player to bend his head down awkwardly to see the ball.

Cutting the Short Putts. How can a golfer eliminate the tendency to pull the short putts off the line to the left of the cup? To conquer this fault, start practicing on a two- or three-foot putt. Follow the 1-2-3-4 swing pattern as already prescribed, but when swinging the club through on Step No. 4, deliberately draw the club across the line of the putt as if trying to produce a slice. This "cut" across the line of the shot keeps the face of the putter square with the direction. Of course, doing this requires a bit of body action, and it is not harmful to exaggerate the movement for a while.

This plan is similar to the old suggestion of hitting against a straight left leg, but it will keep the putter face in perfect line all the way through the swing, and the ball will click off the club and run straight into the cup. It is a definite cure for hooking on the short putts.

Reverse Overlap Grip. In this grip, the overlap is reversed, that is, instead of the little finger of the right hand riding on top of the forefinger of the left hand, the forefinger of the left hand is on top of the little finger of the right hand. This grip has all the fingers of the right hand on the club, and the purpose of this is to give complete control to the right hand. Although the reverse overlap is used quite commonly, I do not recommend it, for too much right hand in putting is just as bad as too much right hand in any other golf stroke. The hands should work in unison, and the stroke to cultivate is a long, sweeping, backhand action with the left hand as the club is swinging through. Good, natural follow-through comes from left hand control, not from the right hand.

FIVE

The Mental Side of Golf

THE GAME OF GOLF IS A PERFECTLY NATURAL GAME TO PLAY, AND IT is one that is easy to learn. Unfortunately, however, many people make golf difficult to learn, principally through their failure to understand the procedures used. Most often, the inability to succeed in golf stems from a lack of comprehension rather than from a lack of the proper physical equipment in the player. For example, people who excel in other sports do not always perform as well on the golf course.

Whether the failure to understand golf can be blamed on the players, for failing to make the necessary effort or take the time to learn, or whether it can be that the game is presented to them in a confusing manner, will not be discussed here. The author will simply try to clear away some of the cobwebs to help lead the reader to a more understandable and consequently more enjoyable game.

Understanding the Game

As a rule, men are inclined to create problems for themselves on the golf course. This is one of the reasons for their failure to make good pupils. The average male becomes egotistical because of the success he has attained in mastering the complexities of life's battle. He has had to work hard to attain his position, so when it comes to golf, he is inclined to want to take it in his stride. Why should he stop to make a problem of the simple matter of playing a game, particularly something as simple as hitting a ball with a stick? Many a strong, virile, brilliant man has become fouled up on a golf course to a point where disappointment, irritation, and confusion cause him to give up the game in disgust. Knowledge of a few elementary facts could have prevented this situation.

Women players, on the other hand, are inclined to depend too much on others for guidance, and they fail to work out in their own minds an aggressive plan of action, so necessary in the game of golf. Because women are good pupils, however, they do develop good form and good golf style, and they really become comparatively better players than their stronger male competitors.

You're On Your Own. Golf, because of its very nature, demands understanding on the part of the player. As we noted in an earlier chapter, golf is unlike most games in that it is played with a still ball. In practically every other game, the ball is put into motion, usually with an intentional deception. Consider, for example, the serve in tennis, the pitch in baseball, or the pass in football. In these sports, if the player does not have the intuition to sense the play or the instinctive ability to get into position for the play, he soon finds himself sitting on the bench.

There is no deceptive delivery in golf, and there is no opposing player to interfere with the play. The ball is on the ground, waiting for the player to act, and the player can take as long as he wants, use whatever club he desires, and follow any method or style he chooses.

So, why shouldn't golf be easy? However, this free choice of time, equipment, and style is the very thing that proves so often to be the undoing of the golfer. Uncertain of the club selected, and perhaps a bit more uncertain of the manner in which he is going to use it, the player has a tendency to become deliberate and doubtful. In short, he develops a mental block and a physical tension which destroy his confidence and his ability to execute the shot.

Planning Your Playing. Golf, because it is a game that is played with a still ball, requires a definite plan or style of action on the part of the player. Although the lie or position of the ball does not always find it setting on top of a nice tuft of turf, at least it is still, and relatively in the same position to the player on every shot. In games other than golf, the ball is not always in the same relation to the player, and he must act instinctively for this reason. But in golf, the player trains himself to act routinely. He develops a style, a definite plan of action, and he needs this plan to start and finish each shot consistently.

No one should rush into golf. A plan should be worked out, and when this is done, an understanding of what to do and how to do it soon develops the confidence essential to good performance. By placing himself under the guidance of PGA professionals, a player will hasten results and guarantee performance.

Confidence and Relaxation

A most important necessity in any undertaking is an attitude of confidence. This is particularly true in golf, because the player must depend on his own efforts to produce a desired result or effect. Confidence is not something that can be assumed. It is not something that a person can wrap around himself as he would a cloak. Confidence is a state of mind that can only be developed through thought and study. When someone thinks a thing through so that he thoroughly understands it from every angle, then he has gained a knowledge of that thing. It is a knowledge of what is required, how to do what is required, and most important, that he himself can perform what is required. Once this is accomplished, confidence is his. Demonstrations of his ability to produce the desired results will cultivate more confidence in the person, and therefore it can be retained indefinitely.

Confidence, therefore, is the result of knowledge, and knowledge, as far as golf is concerned, is of three phases—what to do, how to do it, and proving to yourself that you can consistently produce the desired result. Until you prove it to yourself, you can never have the confidence necessary for a good performance. In this respect, you can fool a lot of people, but you can't fool yourself. It can't be done. The only way confidence can be acquired is through thought, study, and practice.

Once confidence is developed, relaxation is a natural consequence of it. Relaxation is a prime requisite in any physical endeavor, but it comes only through confidence. In a game such as golf, where judgment, direction, a delicacy of swing on short shots, and a speed of motion on power shots are necessary, the successful performer must always be at ease and relaxed.

There are two types of relaxation in golf. One is the strictly muscular type, the kind that depends upon the mechanics of the physical movements that constitute the swing. The other is mental relaxation, the proper frame of mind, and it develops from the confidence we have been discussing. Of course, if the physical mechanics are incorrect, no amount of urging, no amount of practice, is going to do any good. But when one knows what to do and how to do it, and when the physical aspects of the swing are correct, then progress can be made. In all physical performances, there are certain levels of learning, just as there are grades in school. It is the same in golf. Each phase is a natural, orderly sequence of development. Confidence and relaxation—two things all good golfers must acquire.

Teaching to Two. Whenever it is possible or practical, I prefer to teach two people at the same time, with one pupil sitting on the bench and listening to what is being said. This gives each pupil a chance to work the pattern out thoroughly in his mind before trying to execute something he does not understand clearly. This is one of the problems encountered in teaching golf. People are out trying to do something before they know thoroughly what they are supposed to do. It is no wonder that they get all fouled up in their movements and develop so many bad habits that the game becomes difficult or unnatural. Practice is of no value unless the player understands what he is to do. A little PGA guidance can be very helpful in this respect.

The Mental Side of Learning. The author is reminded of a certain lady who, because she was left-handed, felt that golf lessons would not do her any good and that she just had to work it out for herself. She practiced for hours at a time, and one day during a lengthy practice session the weather turned warm, the lady returning to the clubhouse completely exhausted. From her appearance it was evident she was having difficulties. Hoping to give her some encouragement, I asked how her practice had developed.

"Well, Joe," she replied, "I accomplished one thing today for sure. I've reached a definite conclusion. I'm convinced that my clubs have rubber handles and I'm playing with an iron ball."

Here we have one mental aspect that can be developed in golf. This left-handed lady golfer is not alone with the idea that it is the clubs and the ball that go wrong.

Another peculiar quirk was related by a national golf champion when he, among many others, was asked to submit a series of questions and answers on the game, a national newspaper service using the results in a syndicated column. The question of playing a *fade* was brought up—*fade* being the technical term used to designate a shot in which the ball is deliberately curved to the right. A fade is employed to curve the ball around an obstacle such as a tree, and it is a shot that stops very quickly on landing.

The description this winner of a national championship gave on how to play a fade shot was interesting. "When I want to play a fade," he wrote, "I simply *think* a fade. Furthermore," he continued, "if I want to play a hook (curving the ball to the left), I simply *think* a hook. That proves to me," he concluded, "that golf is entirely mental. So if you want to play a good game of golf, simply have confidence in yourself and go to it."

On first analysis, this idea may appear rather weird, but here are the facts in the case. This golfer started to play the game as a youngster, and like a lot of other players, he acquired the knack of hitting a golf ball entirely by imitation. He actually did not learn to play golf—he just grew up with it. He was accustomed, no doubt, to handling and swinging a golf club for many hours each day. As a consequence, he developed a sense and feel of the club, and from experience he learned that a certain way of handling the club produced a slice and another maneuver resulted in a hook. It was second nature for him to move the club to the position which would give him the desired result each time. For this golfer, the game really was entirely mental. He played by habit pattern, and did not try to explain how he positioned the club to get a slice or a hook. With no lessons or instructions, he acquired a golf game entirely through imitation, and executed his good golf shots completely by instinct.

This method of learning golf is not available to everyone. It is possible to acquire the knack of a golf swing through imitation, but this ability to imitate generally is restricted to youngsters, for it takes a long time to learn the game this way. In addition, if the knack gained through imitation is lost, it is quite easy to become confused and never regain proficiency.

The Positive Formula

The only sure way to learn how to play good golf is to follow the method as prescribed in this book. Remember to (a) learn what to do, (b) learn how to do it, and (c) practice until you can successfully reproduce the operation. In this way, the physical as well as the mental aspects of the game can be developed, and the player will always know where he stands and "what the score is."

A 13-year-old girl who took lessons as I suggest was taught what to do and how to do it, and after several instruction periods she began to hit the ball naturally and quite well for a novice. During one of these lessons, she played a drive that sliced to the right quite badly.

"Well, what happened there?" I asked.

"Oh, my club just got off the beam," she replied. "Please let me have another ball."

This incident proves the value of having a plan and understanding that plan. Here was a girl who did not get upset because she happened to miss a shot. She knew exactly what caused the error, and all she wanted was another ball to prove that she could drive a straight shot. This attitude in golf can be developed only when the person has a positive approach to the game.

My advice to anyone who is a newcomer to golf is this: Don't rush your way into the game. Golf is a game that you can play and enjoy all your life, but you must take a little time to learn the few things that one must know. There really is so little to learn that it's a shame to miss the boat. Don't get all bound up physically and wound up mentally, because golf is not that difficult.

What to Practice

As we learned previously, there is only one swing in golf, and the various shots or effects are produced by using the different clubs. It is all a matter of learning the correct stroke, and if the player follows the steps as outlined here, the correct stroke will be the result.

The important things to know are how to stand, how to aim the shot, and how to hold the club. They can be acquired easily by practicing the first four steps:

STEP NO. 1: Place the club to the ball with the left hand.
STEP NO. 2: Adjust the feet to their proper places.
STEP NO. 3: Relax the right knee to complete the grip.
STEP NO. 4: Turn the right heel out.

After the player can carry out these four steps naturally and without any mental or physical difficulty, he will find that he is poised automatically on his left foot each time he completes these steps. The position assumed will be identical with the one he will be in at the moment of impact between the clubhead and the ball. In effect, the player has taken aim as to exactly what position he will be in when the club meets the ball.

Into the Swing. When balanced on the left foot, the player will find that all sense of swing or club movement is impossible unless the weight is shifted to the right foot for the backswing and returned to the left foot for the downswing. After practicing the first four steps to assume the correct position for the shot, the next thing to learn is the actual footwork, whereby the weight is shifted to the foot being pivoted upon.

The correct movements in the backswing and downswing can be developed easily by following the second series of four steps of our routine:

STEP NO. 1: Start the swing with a forward press, a slight forward motion of the knee which will rock the hands forward an inch or two.

STEP NO. 2: Rock the club back by reversing the position of the knees. This will shift the weight to the right foot.

STEP NO. 3: Swing the club away and up from the ball with a pivot motion by drawing the right hip back in a manner similar to the act of throwing.

STEP NO. 4: Allow a slight hesitation at the top of the swing, partially shifting the weight to the left foot. Then reverse the body pivot by drawing the left hip back, exerting a pull on the left arm and bringing the club down and through the ball.

In the first four steps, practice getting the right stance, grip, and position to the ball. In the second four steps, practice shifting the weight to the right foot to start the backswing with a sense of body control, and then practice shifting the weight back to the left foot to obtain the proper body pivot to bring the club into the ball. These two series of four steps get the player in the correct starting position and give him the correct rhythm to develop the footwork and weight shift so essential to a free, full, natural movement of the body. The result is a good golf swing.

Only one thing more needing to be added to this combination of motion is the part the hands play in directing the shot by determining the position of the club throughout the swing. The chapter on HANDS deals more comprehensively with this aspect of the game.

The fundamentals of a good golf swing are:

a. *Proper grip, stance, and starting position.*

b. *A sense of footwork, through which the body pivot is possible.*

c. *The body pivot itself, which actually is the swing because it is what makes the club swing.*

d. *The action of the hands in directing the club throughout the swing.*

These fundamentals are the requirements for the player who wants to develop a good swing, and any PGA golf professional can assist him greatly in acquiring and establishing them. Personally, the author believes that the numbered system, as we have explained it, is absolutely necessary in learning and in teaching the golf swing. The swing is a combination of footwork, body pivot, and hand action, and by use of this numbered system, the operations can be identified and at the same time coordinated into action in a properly-timed rhythmic flow of power.

How to Practice

After you have clearly acquired an understanding of what to do and how to do it, the next thing is to put what you have learned into practice. Therefore, the golfer should go to a practice area and start getting the form he has studied into effect. This should be done on a small scale at first, the player starting off with a No. 7 iron and playing short shots to a distance of from 30 to 50 yards.

When the weight shift, hand action, and body pivot can be executed successfully, longer shots may be attempted. As the results obtained become consistent, the player should gradually work his way up the scale of clubs, practicing with a No. 5 iron, then a No. 3, and so on. In starting to work with the woods, he should be sure to start with the No. 4 wood, taking the No. 3 next, and gradually working up to the No. 1 wood, the driver.

The reason for starting with the more-lofted clubs is that it gives the player a chance to perfect the footwork and weight shift operations first, then the body pivot, and finally the hand action. With the less-lofted clubs, a No. 2 iron or a No. 1 wood, for example, the field of operation as far as the hands are concerned is very limited. What might produce a fair result with a more-lofted club often results in a complete miss with the less-lofted club. For this reason, it is wiser to use the more-lofted clubs in learning. As satisfactory results are produced, confidence is developed and progress becomes faster.

In our present day professional tournament circuit, the stars practice from one to two hours daily. They hit between 100 and 200 shots before actually going to the first tee to begin their game.

The Bobby Jones Practice Plan. Bobby Jones, the Grand Slam champion, who earned the title by winning both the amateur and open championships of the United States and Great Britain within a one-year period, had a unique practice plan that got results. Jones started his practice session by hitting a few balls with the No. 9 iron. Then he concentrated on hitting two perfect shots in succession with this club, and when that was done he put the club back into the bag. He continued this pattern, taking a few shots with the No. 8 iron and then concentrating on hitting two perfect shots in succession with that club. This procedure was followed with every club in the set.

You could say that the purpose of this plan was to give confidence as well as practice. Regardless of what club Jones decided to use for a certain situation during the game, he remembered that the last two shots he played with that club were perfect shots. This gave him every confidence that the club was OK and working well. Consider what may have happened if the situation was reversed. Suppose Jones missed several shots with each of his clubs. Obviously, the clubs would not feel right, because when shots are being missed the club is definitely out of position, and it feels out of balance and awkward.

The player should go to the practice tee and get acquainted with his clubs, practicing with them and getting used to them. By doing this before each game, he will make better scores and enjoy his game more.

Remember, above all, that the golfer who learns what to do, how to do it, and then proves to himself that he can produce the desired results consistently is the one least likely to encounter the mental hazards which plague so many players.

SIX

The Hands in Golf

ONE OF MY CLOSEST FRIENDS WAS FRANK SWEENY, OF THE FAMOUS Sweeny family that made things hum in Couer d'Alene, Idaho, New York, and London. Frank was educated at Harvard. He started golf as a youngster and was always a fairly low handicap player, but he never could perform quite to his own satisfaction.

One day he accosted me on the first tee with these words, "Why is it that when I step up on this first tee and make a few practice swings I feel and apparently look like a million bucks, but when I get to the eighteenth green I'm not worth thirty cents?"

"It's all very apparent," I answered. "You have good footwork

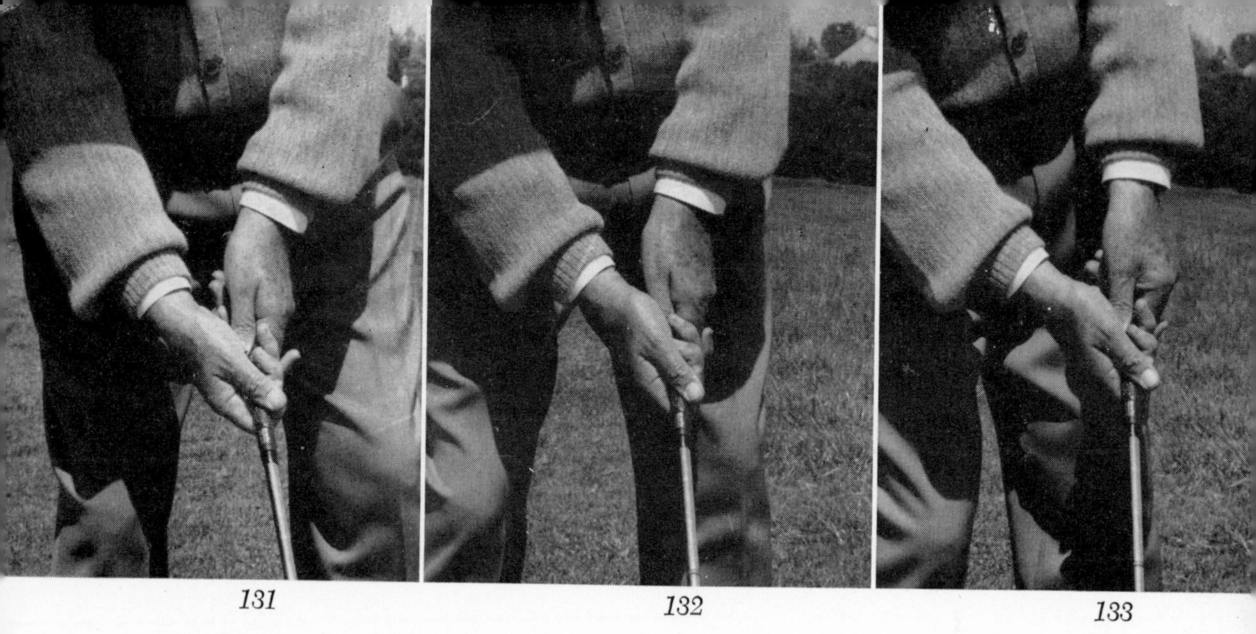

131 132 133

and a good pivot, both of which make for poise, balance, and rhythm. This looks good in a practice swing when there's no ball, but you just don't work your hands right. Therefore your club is never steady or under control, so you drive the ball any place but where you would like to have it go."

Frank Sweeny was no different than the average American boy. In fact, he was rather typical of boys in this country—he had learned to run, throw a baseball, kick a football, pass a basketball—in short, through a normal run of athletics, he had developed a good sense of footwork. From this basic footwork came a sense of balance, a rhythm, and an ability to employ his body as a means of generating the force necessary to accomplish the task at hand in a perfectly natural manner.

Of course, in most of these activities, there was a singlehandedness of purpose or a freehandedness of operation, as throwing a ball, for example, or punching a bag or kicking a football.

But Frank Sweeny didn't enjoy golf because it didn't come easy and somehow didn't seem natural. Why? Because he was started out with the idea that he had to have an absolutely straight left arm and a death grip with his left hand. It is no wonder he could not swing a golf club like he wanted to. He just wouldn't let it swing—he preferred to choke it to death instead. Frank was not alone in this respect. Too many golfers kill their chances of becoming good

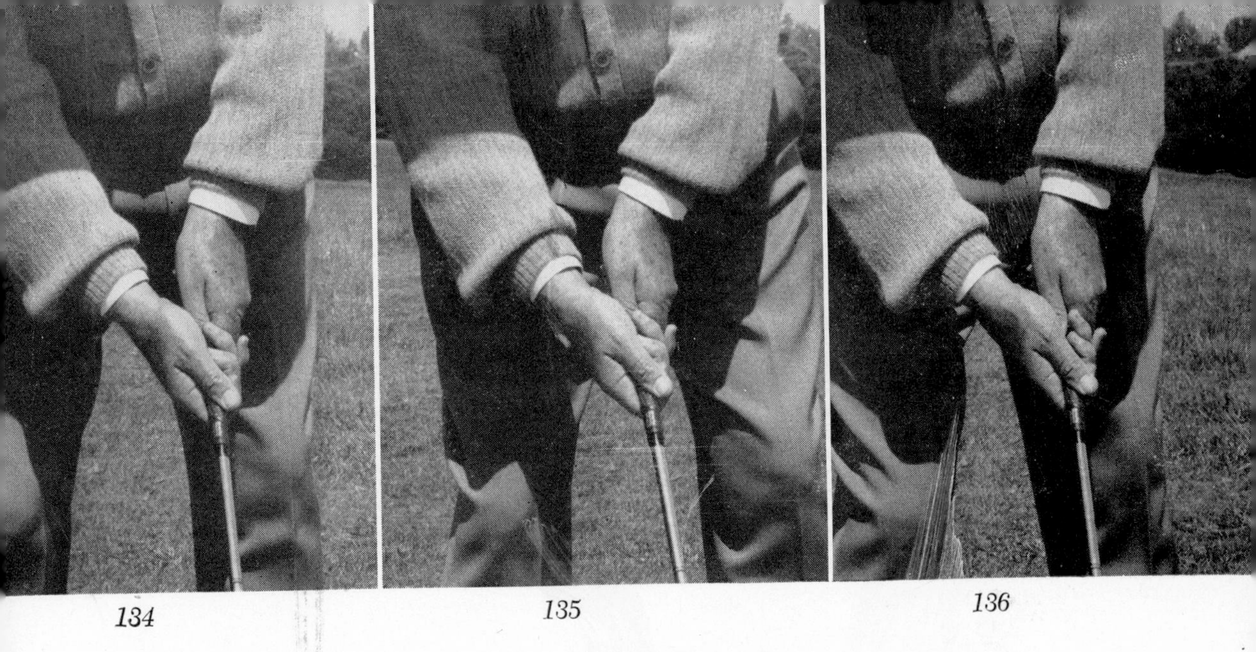

134 135 136

players through the erroneous idea that golf is entirely a one-handed game, an all left-handed game, in which straightness of the left arm and tightness of the left hand are absolutely necessary. This idea has been drilled into them, and nothing could be more harmful.

The Grip

Golf is definitely two-handed and two-fisted. The simplest putt or the easiest chip shot can prove to be an annoying problem unless the golfer knows exactly how to use both hands. The hands must work together. They must aid each other, not defeat each other, in the objective of providing clubhead feel, or a sense of knowing just where the clubhead is throughout the entire swing. In this chapter, it will be possible to thoroughly explain how the hands function in a golf shot so that there can be a sense of understanding

137 138 139

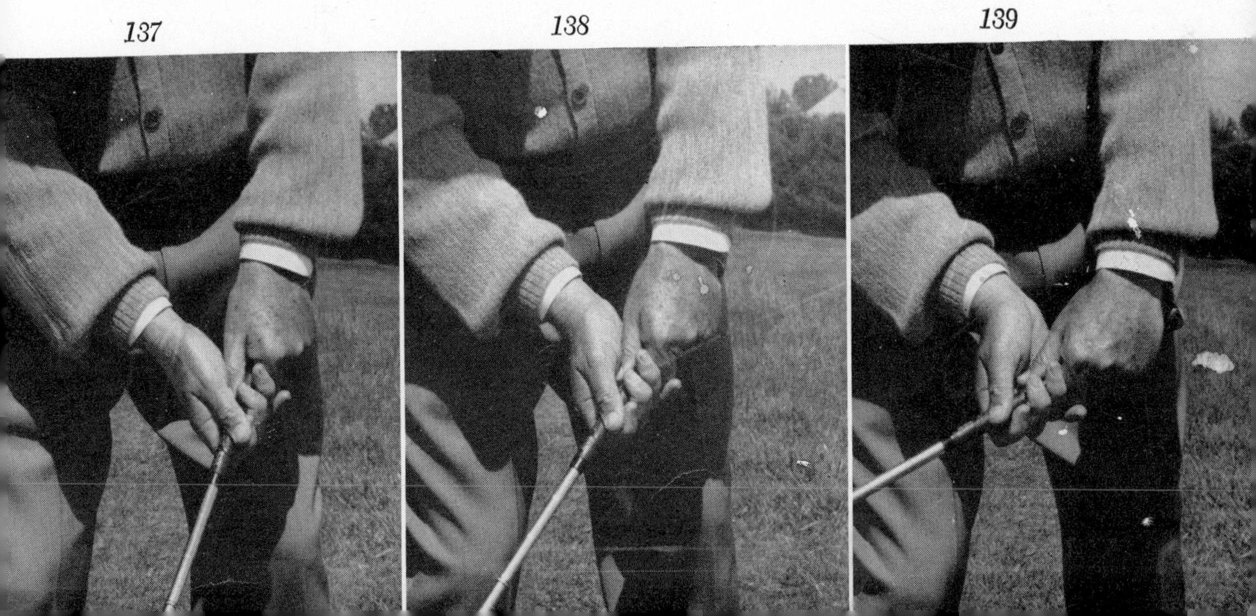

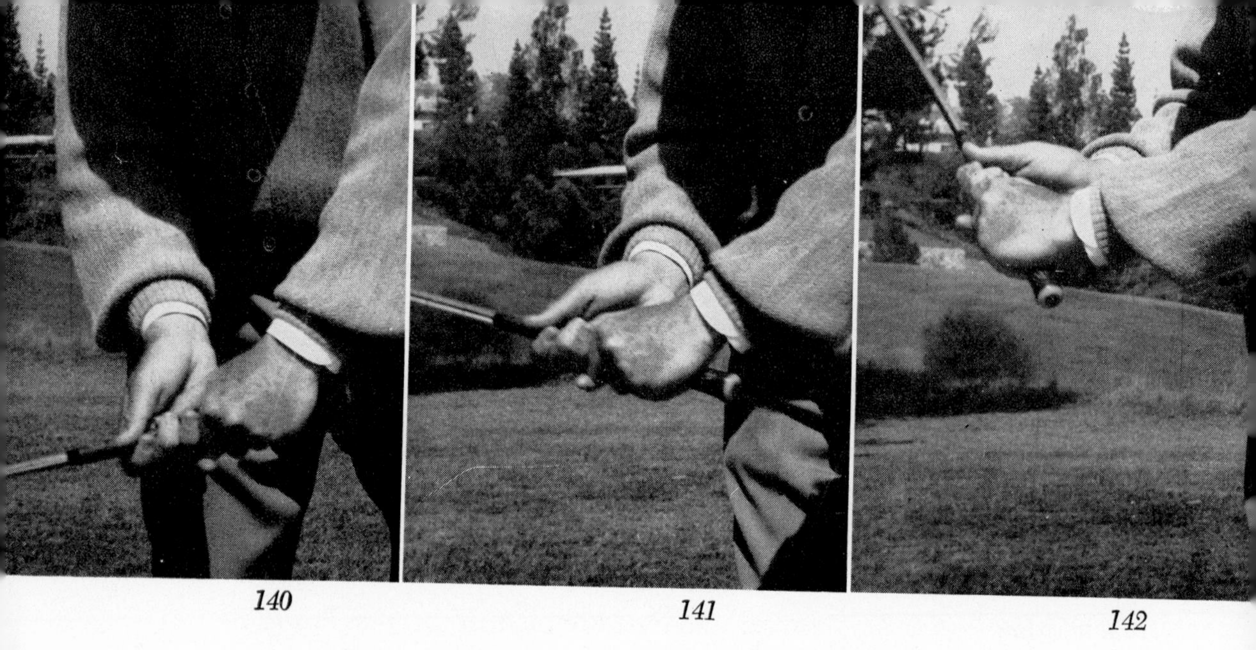

140 141 142

and confidence, a sense of planning and ultimate accomplishment, all of which will result in the fun of making the ball do exactly what the player wants it to do. This, after all, is the real game of golf.

My lengthy experience on the lesson tee has convinced me that golfers do not understand the need of good hand action in a golf shot. Yet, it is with the hands that the club is positioned and maintained in position throughout the swing. What is more, it is through the hands that the power from the body reaches the club. These things cannot be done with tense, tight hands.

Using the Overlapping Grip. Consider for a moment the overlapping grip, by far the most widely used grip in golf. The overlapping grip is the most popular grip because it is the most effective placement of the hands on the club. In the accompanying pictures of this grip, note how the hands are naturally opposed to each other. The right hand is placed so that it can initiate a movement of the

143 144 145

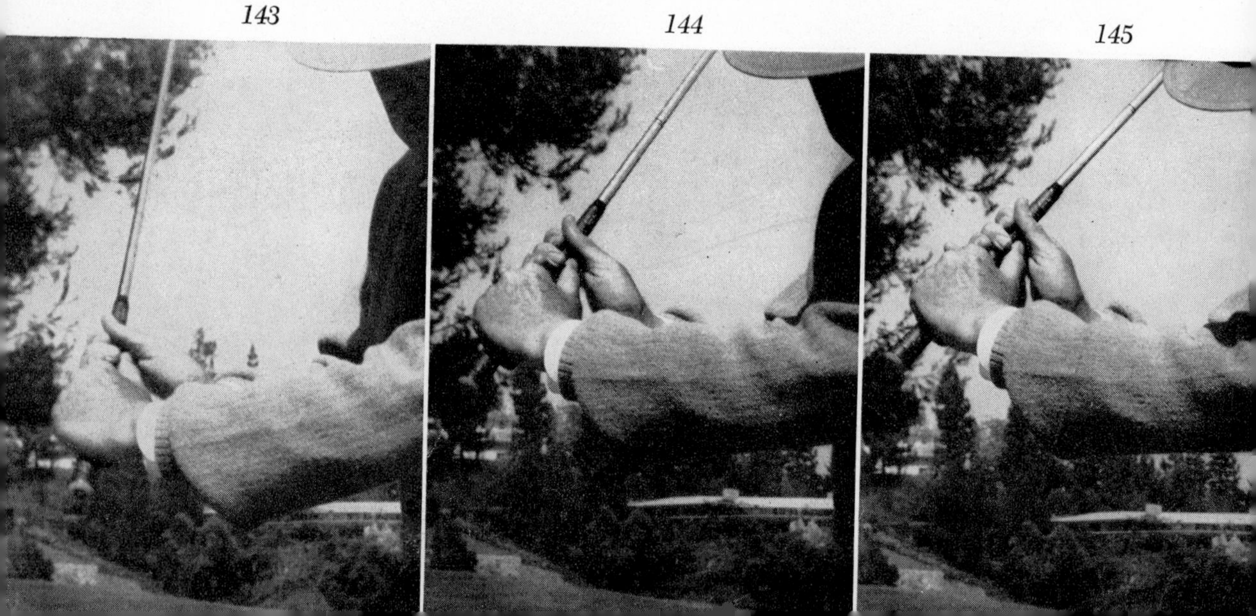

club with the first two fingers and the thumb of that hand. The thumb of the left hand is placed so deeply into the palm of the right hand that it can oppose any action on the part of the right hand. The little finger of the right hand has been eliminated from the grip, and it merely rides on top of the left forefinger in an absolutely relaxed manner.

A sense of not using the little finger of the left hand should be cultivated also, thereby concentrating and centering the grip in the first two fingers and the thumbs of both hands. The thumb positions are most important, because when the top of the swing is reached and the hands are relaxed and extended to their utmost, it is the thumbs that provide the needed guidance and support.

The thumbs apparently are more of an asset than many people realize, despite the old saying that when a person is clumsy his "fingers are all thumbs today." A person being interviewed on a television show not long ago stated that there were two theories about flying saucers. This man, who said he was a scientist studying flying saucers, said that one school of thought believes that the saucers are not real but merely a refractory light arrangement in the sky. The other theory, and the man himself held this opinion, says that they are objects from other planets carrying humans who are trying to make contact with the earth. When asked what he meant by "humans," the scientist answered that they had thumbs like we have.

Apparently, our thumbs have distinguishing characteristics. They are of distinguished importance in the golf swing, too, but

146 147 148

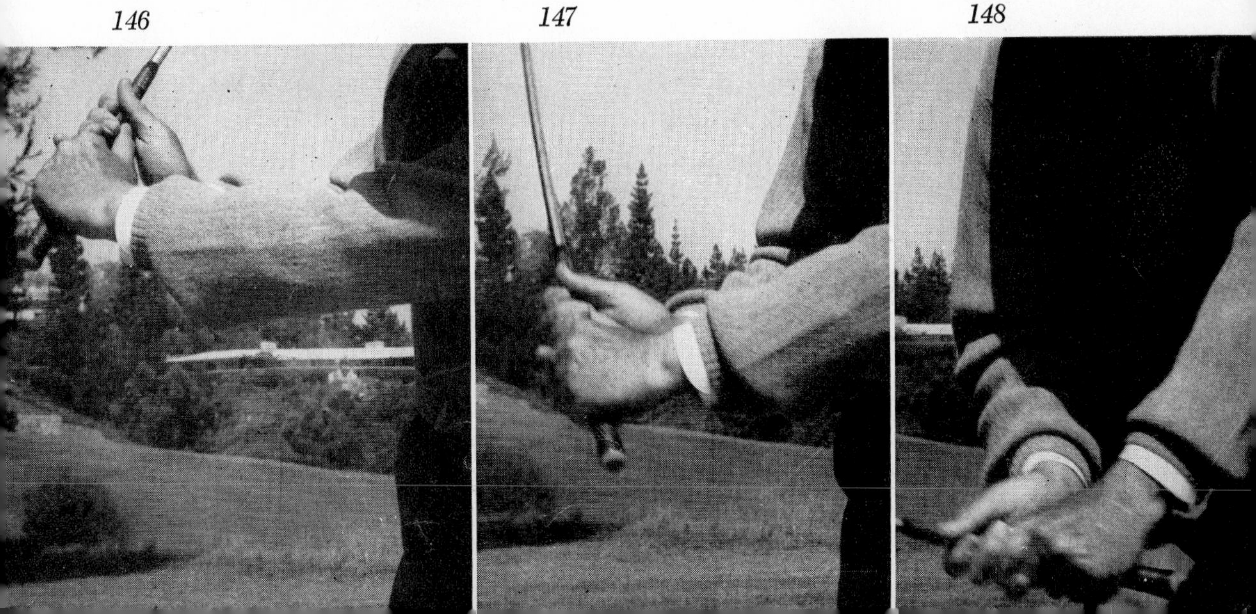

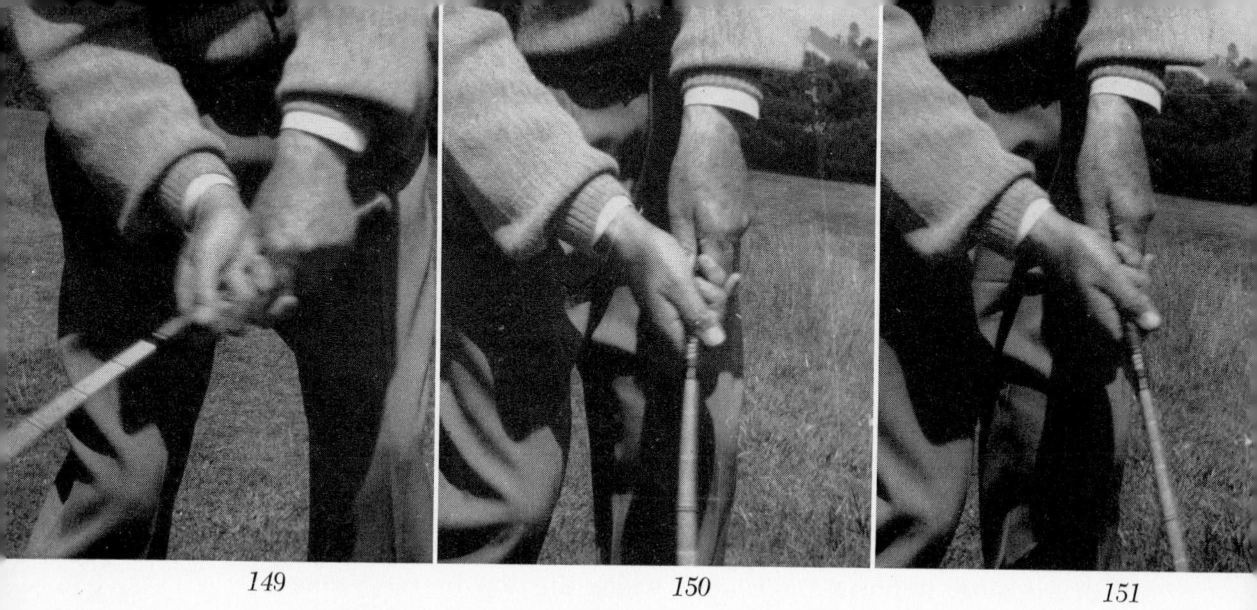

149 150 151

many golfers, because they lock or tighten up the last three fingers of each hand, thereby immobilize their thumbs.

Positioning the Club

The research laboratory of A. G. Spalding & Bros. released a series of pictures some time ago on Bobby Jones' golf swing. In commenting on the pictures, Jones made the statement, "The pictures clearly illustrate a peculiarity of my own which is not recommended by all instructors. In the topmost position it will be seen that the fingers of the left hand have opened perceptibly. For me, this helps to assure a full cocking of the wrists and eases the strain on the hands." This statement coincides with the author's explanations of hand action, and it explains indirectly why so many golfers develop blisters when they play the game. These players simply grab onto the club too tightly, resisting the natural movement of the club and thereby causing friction on the hands.

Learning a Lesson. A gentleman from out of town came to me for a one-hour golf lesson not long ago. He had played for many years, but had always had much difficulty with his woods and was almost ready to give up using them. His iron shots were not entirely satisfactory either, but he could get the ball away most of the time.

Upon watching this man hit a few balls, I noticed that he had absolutely no sense of footwork or weight shift. Naturally, there was no pivot or body turn. This player simply raised the club as best he could with the left arm and returned it to the ball in like fashion with the right arm. Most of his shots were topped, smothered, or driven right into the ground. With this type of motion, wood clubs were ineffective. Only an iron club, one with some loft on the face of it, could get the ball away.

It was pointed out to this man that there were two things he had to learn: (1) a sense of body pivot with which to swing the club, which must be accompanied by an underlying sense of footwork or weight shift, and (2) a sense of hand action to control the club as it is being swung with the body. Obviously, the correct grip, stance, and body position are required to do these things, so it was a case of starting right at the beginning with the first four steps we described earlier.

A repetition of these moves very soon taught the player how to get into the right position for the swing. Then I took over and asked my pupil to watch me hit a few balls.

"Notice that I start with my weight on my left foot," I told him. "With a forward press of the right knee and then a reverse action of the knees, I shift my weight to my right foot, and then I raise the club to the top of the swing with a body turn on my right leg, induced by a backward pull on my right hip. I bring the club on down and through the ball by shifting my weight to my left foot and reversing the body turn by drawing my left hip back."

After going through the swing several times, I repeated it for my

152

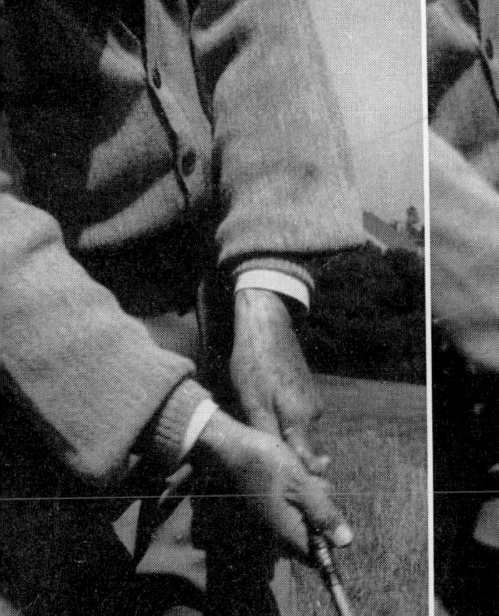

153

154

pupil "by the numbers," using the 1-2-3-4 series of steps we learned for the swing in previous chapters. Further explanation was needed to get across the idea of the sleight of hand performance with which the golfer guides and sets the club so that he knows exactly how it is aimed and where the ball will fly. It was explained in detail how the hands cock the club at the outset of the backswing, and from this demonstration the pupil learned an entirely new technique of striking a golf ball. This player was taught the necessary footwork, how to carry the club up and down through the swing with pivot control, and above all, how to work the hands at the start of the backswing to get a definite feel and control over the club before making the swing.

Getting the Feel of the Club

The good golfer always gets a preliminary "feel" of the club before he hauls off into the swing. In fact, experienced players try out their hand action with the club once, twice, or even several times before they swing. They don't swing until the club feels right in the hands, for they know this goes a long way toward determining whether or not the shot will be successful. Watch any good golfer and you will see a forward press motion of the right knee to start off the movement. A reverse press usually follows, and then the hands act to give the club the distinctive set-up action at the start of the backswing.

Jimmy Demaret made the following statement just after winning

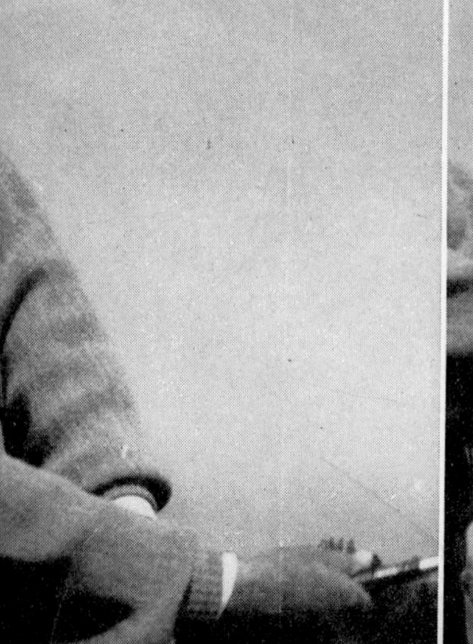

the 1950 Masters Golf Tournament at Augusta. "To increase my backswing," he said, "I have evolved what George Fazio calls the *triple press.* Most players use what we call a *forward press* to get into motion.

"First I press the clubhead on the ground, directly behind the ball. Then without changing the clubhead position, I start my hands forward a couple of inches, then my body follows in a slight shift. Then I start my hands back, then my body, and I am in motion on the swing after the triple press. It has helped to give me a smooth, relaxed swing, and I think it is the key to my longer driving and my recent success."

Picturing the Hands at Work. The accompanying series of pictures shows exactly how the hands work at the outset of the backswing to position the club. Although the good golfer almost always makes a false start with the club to test its position, this hand action is difficult to follow because it occurs simultaneously with the backswing and is almost, as we have said, a sleight of hand action. However, when separated from the swing itself, as in these pictures, this process can be seen and more clearly understood. Remember, it all takes place within an area of 45 degrees from the starting position.

The Push-Pull Action

The action of the hands in a golf shot is one of a pull and push type. This holds true in all shots, including long and short drives, iron shots, or even putting. On the backswing, as the body turns to the right, the right arm pulls on the club while the left arm pushes. On the downswing, the left arm pulls and the right arm pushes. The thumbs have a great responsibility in this action, because they provide the fulcrum points for the movement.

Under such a push-pull action, there must be a natural expansive movement by the hands themselves, as suggested by Bobby Jones. This does not mean that the fingers ever let go of the club, but that they have an easy, firm grip without the slightest trace of tenseness.

Any undue tension or tightness in the hands is bound to create friction and produce blisters. Most beginners, particularly women, are inclined to grasp the club handle much too tightly.

Learning to Relax the Hands. As a means of getting these people to relax, I call their attention to the fact that a golf club weighs less than a pound. A 15-ounce club is fairly heavy. I suggest that they take 7½ ounces of the club in their right hand and 7½ ounces in the left hand. The knowledge that they are carrying less than a half a pound in each hand seems to help break up the tenseness of the grip.

To get the proper feel of the club at the outset of the backswing, a good practice idea is to assume the position to start a swing, do the one-two moves of the forward press and reverse press, and when the weight has been shifted to the right foot, take the left hand off the club completely. Remain in this position, with the weight on the right foot, and pick the club up from the ball using the right arm only. Raise the club up in this manner three or four times, each time resting the right elbow on the right hip. After three or four such pick-ups with the right hand, insert the left thumb at its proper point on the shaft and learn to kick or tilt the clubhead to the 45-degree point as illustrated in the pictures.

By doing this, the player is first training the right hand in its phase of the operation, and then training the left hand to carry out its part. Although both hands are necessary and indispensable in the club-positioning routine, the left hand obviously is the creative medium. It is within the power of the left hand to either open or close the club, thereby determining what type of shot will be made.

Knowing this, many golfers have placed undue emphasis on left-hand control, and some have interpreted this as meaning there should be a tenseness or tightness in the grip. This is unfortunate, for nothing has caused so many bad shots in golf as not knowing how to work the left hand. This also is the basic cause of that curse of golf—shanking. Here's hoping these pictures and this chapter will present a new outlook.

Hand Action in Pictures

Illustration 131 shows the address at the ball, using the overlapping grip. Note the slight tilt of the club handle in the direction of the shot, the point midway between the hands being directly over the ball.

The forward press is pictured in Illustrations 132–133. Notice the relaxed position of the hands, and how, through a forward motion of the right knee, the club handle has been pushed into the left hand. The hands now are at a point ahead of the ball.

Illustrations 134–136 show the reverse press. By reversing the knee position and shifting the weight to the right foot, the hands are swung back toward the right knee, and the club handle is thrown into the right hand. The left hand is relaxed and has no direct influence on the club at this point. The hands are almost directly opposite the right knee. The clubhead is still on the ground at the ball.

This is where the hands start their important task of establishing a position or set of the club. Illustrations 137–138 show a distinct lift of the club with the right hand, while the left arm relaxes, the elbow bent slightly. In Illustrations 138–139, the downward counter action of the left hand takes place, principally through the medium of the left thumb, not by any pressure from the back or heel of the hand. The downward pressure of the left hand sets or cocks the club in the desired position, determining whether the shot will be straight, a hook, or a slice. The clubhead swings about 45 degrees from the ball, and the hands move back to a spot directly over the ball.

The backswing is pictured in Illustrations 140–145, a pivot of the body bringing the club from its 45-degree position from the ball to the top of the swing. Under the influence of the body pivot, the right arm retains its bent position and the left arm reaches an extended, full-length position in keeping the club cocked or set. Illustration 145 shows the club at the top of the swing.

Illustrations 146–150 picture the downswing, which is started with a shift of the weight to the left foot. The left hip draws back, producing a natural pull-the-bell-cord action in the left arm, the back of the left hand being drawn right down on the ball.

Impact of the clubhead with the ball is shown in Illustration 150. The left arm pulls, and the right hand aids by pushing on the club handle. Illustrations 151–157 show the follow-through, with the complete turn on the left foot. Notice the straight thrust of the right arm at the impact point.

SEVEN

The Slice and Hook Shots

THE SHORTEST DISTANCE BETWEEN TWO POINTS IS A STRAIGHT LINE, and the ideal way to play a golf shot is to drive it on a straight line right into the cup. Nevertheless, there are times on the golf course when it becomes necessary to bend a shot around a tree. Other times, the terrain is such that it is advantageous to play a high shot with a *break* to the right or a low shot with a *run* to the left.

Experts play such shots as many as three out of four times in a round, and the amazing part of it is that these shots are not anywhere near as difficult as they appear to be. The successful execution of such a shot often spells the difference between success and

158

159

160

failure in a tournament. In match play, these shots can demoralize an opponent, and by making them when they are needed, the player receives a feeling of confidence and aggressiveness.

Making a Recovery

Spectators at the Los Angeles Open golf tournament in 1950 saw two spectacular shots recorded within the space of an hour on the same hole. The eighth hole, a tricky 370-yard affair, elbows slightly to the right and has a very narrow fairway. To the right of the fairway is a deep ravine, and both sides of the fairway are lined with tall eucalyptus trees.

Lawson Little, former American and British Amateur champion, pushed his drive off into the ravine to the right. His ball lay fairly well, but directly between him and the green, which was 160 yards away, were the trees and a steep bank. However, there was an opening directly to the left, and Little decided to play a low slice shot into this opening. Using a No. 3 wood to get a good "bite" on the ball, Little executed the shot perfectly, and his ball started out to the left. After travelling about 100 yards, it turned sharply to the right and finished up on the green, where Little scored an easy par.

161

162

163

About an hour later, Sam Snead poled out one of his prodigious drives, but it wound up about 20 yards off the fairway to the left and almost directly behind one of the tall trees. There was an opening to the right, and Snead elected to play a low hook shot with a No. 6 iron. The ball started out just as he intended. It shot out through the opening to the right and then did a perfect turn to the left. It hit on the front of the green and stopped eight feet from the cup, from where Snead sank his putt to score a birdie three.

From the standpoint of making recovery shots, we can see that it is necessary to be able to slice and hook at will. There is another aspect to this slice and hook business, however. Unless the player knows exactly what makes the ball fly crookedly or "off the line," he certainly cannot do much about making it fly straight. The purpose of this chapter is to show how easily slices and hooks can be played. And, from learning how to make the ball fly off-center, the player can learn how to keep his shots right on center all the time.

Getting Direction from the Hands

There are but two controlling factors or elements in a golf swing —the *power* or energy, which determines distance, comes from the body pivot, and the *direction* is a result of the positioning of the club

164 165 166

by the hands. Expressing this in another way, let's say that all good golfers have the ability to drive the ball a long way. This comes from one source, and that is from their ability to use the body fully and freely in a natural turn or pivot. Of course, this body pivot requires an underlying sense of footwork or efficiency in shifting the weight.

In addition to being able to get distance, good players have the ability to keep the ball on the line. They have, in other words, the knack of keeping the club in the proper position or relationship throughout the swing, so that the ball will fly as they want it to. Most successful golfers have the skill to hit the ball hard, but they

167 168 169

170 *171* *172*

also are able to deliberately change the position of the club while they are swinging it, making the ball hook, slice, or fly straight, just as they wish.

This is truly the fun of playing golf. It is a perfectly simple matter to hit a golf ball, but to make the ball respond to your wishes —slide to the right, pull to the left, or fly "right down the flagpole" —that is the real art of the game. Through the simple process of establishing a sense of swing with the body, the hands are left free to guide the club to produce the shot desired. Any deviation from this combination of the body pivot for power and the hands for direction can only lead to inconsistent and disappointing results.

173 *174* *175*

When slicing and hooking are being considered, it is natural that attention should be paid to the grip and the stance. Players are cautioned, however, that stance alone, grip alone, or even both of them together, will not necessarily correct a hook or a slice condition, because at best they are contributing influences only.

Influence of the Stance

An open stance foot position so places the body in relation to the direction of the shot that there is an influence toward making the club travel across its normal arc, from "outside to in." Of course, application of the club to the ball in this manner makes the ball start off to the left initially, but there is such a strong spin on the ball from right to left that it is carried far out to the right. Thus, a slice is produced.

In the pictures portraying the closed stance, it can be seen that this foot position tends to make the club swing from "inside to out," and the movement of the club produces the reverse spin on the ball, a spin from left to right. This carries the ball off to the left in a hook.

Stance, therefore, is a strong influence toward making the club swing from outside to in, or from inside to out, but the real determining factor in how the ball is going to fly is the position of the club itself in relation to the direction of the shot. A billiard player want-

179 180 181

ing *reverse english* on the cue ball tilts his cue down, and if he desires a *follow run,* he tilts the cue up so that it meets the upper half of the ball. Similarly, the golfer gets his hooks and slices by positioning his club to make the face meet the ball in a certain manner.

The Slice

When a golfer desires a slice, he simply cocks his club in an open position at the outset of the backswing and maintains the club in that open position throughout the swing. This causes it to come across the ball from outside to in, and a slice shot must result. An open stance, when used with the above procedure, helps to produce the slice.

The Hook

The player reverses the club position for a hook, using a closed swing and making certain to keep the club in this position throughout the swing. The club is bound to swing from inside to out when this procedure is followed, and a hook will be the result. A closed stance aids in producing a hook.

By cocking the club in an in-between position, neither open nor closed, the golfer obtains a perfectly straight shot. Players should

182 183 184

remember this if their shots are turning to the right or left every time. It is the remedy needed to get the shots back in line.

Opening and Closing the Clubface

The ball will be influenced to fly according to the angle of the clubface as it contacts the ball. If the clubface is open, the ball must turn to the right, and if it is closed, the ball must curve to the left. When the clubface is square with the ball at impact, the ball will fly true.

Although this principle of *open club, closed club,* and *square club* has long been recognized in golf, there has not been enough

185 186 187

188 189 190

emphasis placed upon the importance of learning to execute these various positions of the club. Personally, I feel that even before a person gets too serious about swinging a golf club, he should have a definite idea about whether the club is going to be open, closed, or square during the swing. What is the use of swinging the club if the golfer doesn't know the position of it as he swings?

All of this may sound as though it should be something reserved for expert golfers in tournament play, but this business of club position in the golf swing is basic and elemental. In fact, a true understanding of the difference between distance and direction in the swing can come only when the player can distinguish between the swing of the club as one thing, and the position of the club through-

191 192 193

194 195 196

out the swing as another. Many golfers place the club to the ball, lock their hands tight on the club, and then try to maintain that position throughout the swing.

Positioning the Club

The experienced golfer places the club to the ball in the desired position and holds the club lightly in his hands. He starts his swing with a forward press, then makes a reverse press and shifts his weight to the right foot. At this point, he starts his club back with the right hand and cocks it with the left hand. In other words, the good player begins his swing with the 1-2 motion of the knees, and shifts

197 198 199

200 *201* *202*

his weight from the left foot to the right foot. Then, there is a start with the right hand and a cocking motion with the left hand, which flips the clubhead to a 45-degree angle from the ball.

If the player wants to produce a slice, as set action is applied to the club he turns the left hand in toward the body slightly, thereby cocking the club in an open position. In executing the slice, the club shaft is kicked out and away from the player, and the face of the club is turned toward the sky. To produce a hook, the golfer turns his left hand away from the body at the time the club is cocked. This cocks the club in a closed position, because it tilts the shaft to the inside and toward the right toe, and at the same time turns the face of the club toward the ground.

203 *204* *205*

206 207 208

Once the club is cocked—open, closed, or square—the golfer then goes into the swing with his body, maintaining the club in the position it was set, and the desired shot results.

Remember the Rule. Always tilt the club handle to the inside of the line and toward or near the right toe when closing the club. Always tilt the club handle away and outside the line of the shot, away from the right toe, when opening the club.

This positioning of the club is done at the outset of the backswing, before the pivot. Under no condition should the hands carry the clubhead more than 45 degrees from the ball, because it is the body pivot which takes over to bring the club up in the backswing.

209 210 211

212

213

214

Picture Analysis of the Slice

Illustration 158 shows the address to the ball. Notice the stance and the grip. An open stance is used so that the club swings across the line and to the outside on the backswing, and back across the line of the shot to the inside as it comes down and through. In the grip, the left hand is more in front of the handle than on a normal shot, and the right hand is more on top of the shaft than usual. This tends to open the club automatically at the outset of the backswing.

Illustration 159 shows the forward press, and Illustration 160 pictures the reverse press. The pick-up action by the right hand is portrayed in Illustration 161, while the downward, cocking or setting motion of the left hand is shown in Illustrations 162–163. Because a slice is desired in this case, the left hand and wrist turn inward toward the body slightly, cocking the club in an open position. Notice that the club handle is out away from the body and the clubface turned toward the sky.

Illustrations 164–166 show the club being returned to its original position after this preliminary set of the club at the 45-degree point from the ball. Illustration 167 pictures the second setting motion, and the start of the backswing is seen in Illustration 168. The top of the swing is reached in Illustration 173. Notice that the club

215 216 217

shaft is pointing to the left of the line of direction and that the club-face is open.

The downswing is pictured in Illustrations 174–178, and Illustration 179 shows the impact with the ball. Notice that the hands are way ahead of the club in this natural slicing position. Illustrations 180–187 show the follow-through. The hands finish high and off to the left of the line, indicating that the club has drawn across the ball from outside-to-in, producing the slice.

Picture Analysis of the Hook

Illustration 188 pictures the address at the ball for a hook shot. A closed stance is employed, the right foot being drawn back from

218 219 220

221 (left). This is the position for a hook. The left hand is more on top of the shaft and the right hand is turned more under. The right foot is drawn back, and the club is placed to the ball with the club-face slightly open. The shaft is tilted so that the hands are above a point well ahead of the ball. 222 (right) shows the position for a slice. Here the left hand is more in front of the shaft, as is the right hand. Note that the right foot is advanced, and that the ball is played opposite the left foot.

the line of direction. In the grip, the left hand is more on top of the club, and the right hand is more under the shaft, making it easier for the left hand and wrist to turn outward and cock the club in a closed position.

The forward press is shown in Illustration 189, and the reverse press is seen in Illustration 190. Illustrations 191–192 show the

223 (left). With the ball above the feet in a side-hill lie, you have a tendency to hook. The best idea is to aim to the right and "play for the hook." 224 (right) shows a side-hill lie with the ball below foot level. Since this situation usually produces a slice, the best procedure is to aim to the left.

pick-up action of the club by the right hand, and Illustrations 193–194 picture the countering downward action by the left hand, an outward turn of the left wrist and hand cocking the club in a closed position. Notice that the club shaft is tilted to the inside of the line of direction and the face of the club is turned down toward the ground.

Illustrations 195–197 show the club being returned to its original position after the preliminary test of the set or position of the club, and Illustration 198 shows that the club is back in starting position at the ball, and is ready for a repetition of the setting procedure.

Illustration 207 pictures the top of the swing for the hook shot, with the club shaft pointing exactly on the line of the shot and the clubface closed or turned toward the sky. Note the path of the club in the downswing, shown in Illustrations 208–212. It is from the inside to the outside for the hook.

The impact at the ball is shown in Illustration 213, and Illustrations 214–220 portray the follow-through. Compare the low finishing position of the club in this shot with the high finishing position in the slice shot.

EIGHT

Some Typical Case Histories

THE FOLLOWING ARE ACTUAL CASE HISTORY RECORDS OF PUPILS HAVing typical golf problems. In each case, there will be an explanation of the difficulties the pupil encountered, how the situation was analyzed, what remedies were prescribed, and a report of the results accomplished.

Obviously, the worst fault that can be committed in golf is for the player to *fan,* or miss the ball completely. From this, which is strictly a beginner's problem, the cases cited will take the player through the following categories:

1. Fanning the ball
2. Topping the ball
3. Hitting ground behind ball
4. Slicing
5. Hooking
6. Pushing
7. Pulling
8. Hooking-slicing alternately
9. Shanking

It is hoped that by studying the cases presented players having similar problems may find information helpful in remedying their golf faults.

Case No. 1—Fanning the Ball

As we have stated, fanning the ball—that is, missing it completely —is strictly a beginner's fault. It happens, not because the player does not "keep his eye on the ball," but because he has not learned to shift his weight properly, and this prevents him from making the proper pivot or body turn. As a consequence, all that the player is doing is swinging the club with his arms. It will be found that this combination of no weight shift, no pivot, and only arm swing causes the player to swing the club out and over the ball, missing it completely.

Solving the Problem. In cases of fanning, emphasis on *keeping the eye on the ball* or *holding the head still* often complicates the situation further. Such suggestions tend to cause the player to become even more tense than before, and matters may become worse.

Calling for relaxation and less effort has a helpful effect, but the only sure cure is for the player to learn (a) the proper footwork, (b) the correct setting or positioning of the club, and (c) the correct pivot or body turn. When a golfer has these things perfected, he actually can close his eyes and hit the ball well.

225. One of the most common faults of beginning golfers is missing the ball completely. Fanning the ball is the result of an incorrect pivot. In the drawing above I am shown making my pivot improperly—note that my weight has shifted awkwardly to the right foot and my left leg is not flexed. The player who swings this way is just swinging the club with his arms—his body is not contributing to the power of the swing. (See Case History No. 1.)

Case No. 2—Topping the Ball

Not long ago, a 40-year old man came to me for instruction. He was fairly tall, had a good average-type build, but no particular athletic experience. The game was not fun for him, he explained, because he just could not avoid topping the ball. He inferred that his clubs were too short for him, but when it was pointed out that he topped the ball with his wood clubs, which had longer shafts than his iron clubs, he realized that the error was in his swing and not in the clubs.

Analyzing the Swing. An analysis of the player's swing revealed that (a) at the start of the shot he assumed a position with both knees practically straight, (b) the weight was evenly divided on both feet, and (c) because of the straight knee position, he had to bend forward from the waist to get the club near the ball. Bending forward from the waist caused more tension throughout the body, which was already tightened up from the straight knee position. As the swing was made, there was no footwork, no shift of weight, and no pivot action or body turn with which to swing the club away from the ball.

About all the player could do from this stance and this body position was to push the club away from the ball with the left arm. This movement caused the left shoulder to turn forward and made the player straighten up, forcing him to raise the club with the arms. There was no tendency for the left heel to leave the ground on the backswing, and when the top of the swing was reached the net result found the player locked in an off-balance, tilted-toward-the-left-foot position. The only movement possible for the player was to swing forward with the arms only, principally the right arm, causing the club to keep swinging up and over the ball.

It was pointed out to this golfer that there was no footwork or sense of weight shift, no pivot action or body turn, and no regulation or control of the position of the club with the hands.

Prescribing the Remedy. Through the 1-2-3-4 method of get-

226. Here is the beginning of the downswing of a player who habitually tops the ball. The knees are straight and the left shoulder has turned forward. This swing forces the player to straighten up, and on the downswing the club will go up and over the ball. (See Case History No. 2.)

ting set, the player was taught the correct stance, the club and hand positions, and how to balance himself on his left foot at the start of the swing, the same position he would be in at the time the ball was hit.

The player then was shown how to shift his weight to his right foot, enabling him to raise the club from the ball with the pivot motion, which consists mainly in drawing the right hip back to develop a stretch the same way a baseball pitcher does when he winds up. The player found that this was a more natural and effective manner of swinging the club away from the ball than the awkward forward motion of the left shoulder and hip that he had been using.

After the pupil learned to shift his weight to the right foot and could raise the club as prescribed, it was explained to him that he had to reshift his weight to the left foot, so that the motion of the body could be reversed and the club swung through naturally. By the time two lessons on footwork and weight shift had passed by, the player began to connect solidly on approximately every other shot.

Completing the Pattern. In the third lesson, the golfer was shown that at the outset of the backswing it was necessary to apply a sense of control or guidance over the club. The pupil grasped the importance of clubhead control immediately, and learned the sense and feel of club position in a very short time. It was easy to set up the 1-2-3-4 swing pattern, the continuity of motion starting with a shift of the weight to the right foot and progressing with the positioning of the club at the outset of the backswing, the body pivot raising the club to the top of the stroke and the reshifting of the weight to the left foot and the reverse turn of the body bringing the club down and through the ball.

By successive stages, this player learned:

1. The correct position of body, feet, hands, and club.
2. The necessary footwork or weight shift.
3. The proper positioning of the club.
4. The sense of swing with the body.

At the end of four lessons, he had smoothed all of these operations into a rather even combination of movements, and the fault of topping the ball was eliminated entirely. The club was coming into the ball with a good, natural backhand movement with the left arm, and the ball was being met on the downward arc of the swing. Previously, the clubhead had been striking the ball on the upward arc, after the downward arc had been completed.

With his topping fault completely eliminated, this golfer developed a real interest in the game, and his scores dropped from the 120's into the 90's.

Case No. 3—Hitting Ground behind the Ball

The pupil this time was an elderly man who had played a lot of golf, but the divots he removed would do justice to a strong coal-heaver with a big shovel.

A study of this golfer's form revealed that he had good footwork and a good pivot action, but that he was possessed with the idea of starting the club down with a flip of his wrists. This resulted in an early right-handed drive of the club on the downswing. As this was being carried out, the player kept his weight on his right foot, and the natural result of all this was that the club kept hitting the ground behind the ball.

Correcting the Fault. The player was advised that a conscious guiding or cocking of the club should take place at the outset of the backswing, and that once this club position was established, it had to be maintained throughout the swing. An explanation of the necessity of a slight pause at the top of the backswing was made, the pause following Step No. 3 of the swing pattern.

The player learned that this hesitation at the top of the swing gave him time to reshift the weight, at least partially, to the left foot. In addition, he found that the correct movement of the club into the ball with the left side and left arm in control eliminated the right-hand slap at the top of the swing. To establish the pause in the swing, the player was taught to employ a distinct 1-2-3 AND 4

227. The "scooper" is a common figure on any golf course. He has no shift of weight on the downswing, as shown here, and the almost certain result will be a big divot scooped up. Note also that the right hand and right arm are too much in control. (See Case History No. 3.)

rhythm, emphasis on the *and* helping to correct the fault of hitting the ground behind the ball.

Case No. 4a—Slicing

Many golfers have the slicing problem at one time or another during their golfing days. A man with a definite slice came to ask my advice about the difficulty a short time ago. He was about 36 years old, strong, and had been active in baseball and football before taking up golf.

An observation of his swing revealed an extremely stiff, straight left arm and a very tense, tight grip with the left hand during the swing. The grip was especially tight in the last three fingers of the left hand. There was some trace of footwork and knee motion, and consequently some body pivot. However, the pivot was not correct, for there was nothing systematic about it. It looked to be some type of effort to relax or get away from tenseness. The only really certain thing in this man's swing was the death grip with the left hand and the absolutely unbending, rigid left arm.

A Wide Open Club. This golfer was forced to push the club away from the ball with a movement of the left side and left shoulder, as if there were a spike driven from the right shoulder down the right side to the right heel. The entire left side, shoulder, hip, and arm, swung the club away from the ball, and with the tight left-hand grip and stiff left arm, the only thing for the player to do was to roll the club into an open position. Instead of having the club raised or naturally swung to a position with the hands high and the club over, above and across the neck, he was rolling the club around on a very low plane, paralleling a belt position.

With the club wide open and down low around the waistline, the player was pulling across the ball. The slice action was so pronounced that his No. 7 iron shots were actually curving from 30 to to 40 degrees, and that is not easy to do with this club. Of course, his shots had no distance, and it was dangerous to permit him to use

228. Slicing is common to many a golfer's game. There are many causes, but one of the most prevalent is a grip such as I am demonstrating here—sometimes called the "businessman's grip" because it is so common. This grip causes the player to pick the club up with the right hand, since it is over the shaft too much, and the swing that results will mean a slice. (See Case History No. 4a.)

229. With a tight left-handed grip and a stiff left arm, the only thing a golfer can do is roll the club into an open position. This will result in a swing in which the club will pull across the ball and produce a slice. *(See Case History No. 4a.)*

a driver because of the possibility of the ball sweeping around to the right so much that it might come back and hit him.

Cutting Out the Slice. The first thing suggested to get this player back on the right track was a proper shift of the weight to the right foot at the outset of the swing. An emphatic 1-2 rock motion was used with the club to break up the locked position in the left hand and left arm. This was a help in giving the right arm and right hand a chance to function in the backswing. Progress in this case remained fairly slow, so it was suggested that the little finger of the left hand be removed from the club to assist in breaking up the tension in the back of the left hand. At intervals, the little finger was doubled up and curled under the shaft so there could be no tension.

After four lessons, the player developed a good sense of footwork and occasionally some good, straight shots were played. But the tendency to open the club was still present, and although results were fairly satisfactory with the irons, the slicing persisted with the woods. Continued practice on the 1-2-3-4 rhythm established good weight shift and pivot action, but to conquer the tendency to slice, this pupil had to be taught to place his right hand well under the club shaft and to use the right hand and arm in the backswing. This changed the arc of his swing from a low left-handed sweep around the right hip pocket to one starting from the correct high, right-handed position over the right ear.

The emphasis was on the hands in the lessons that followed, and the stressing of the importance of correct clubhead position taught the player how to sense a partially closed club position throughout the swing. Now, drives of 230 and 250 yards replaced the puny 100- and 150-yard pop-ups to the right. The player's scores dropped from the vicinity of 120 down into the 80's. Again it was a matter of teaching footwork, body pivot, and correct club position through the hands.

230. If you have a tendency to shift your weight to the left foot on the backswing, you will probably slice the ball. Here I am demonstrating what happens if you have incorrect balance at the start of the swing. With the right knee in this position at the start of the backswing, the club may very well be raised almost straight up from the ball. This will cause the clubface to be thrown open just before the top of the swing, and, of course, it is probable that a slice shot will result. (See Case History No. 4b.)

Case No. 4b—Slicing

This slicing case involved a man who did a lot of travelling. Golf was his hobby, and he had a strong interest in the game. However, a persistent slice and the attendant loss of distance on his shots made the game quite an effort, and the exertion required to execute his shots made golf seem all work and no fun. His form revealed a good stance, but there was too much tension in the left hand and the right hand was much too far on top of the club handle.

Finding What's Wrong. In the swing, the player started his motion with a slight forward press action with the right knee, but as soon as he concluded this starting move, he raised the club almost straight up from the ball with a tight left hand and a straight left arm. The clubface was thrown into an open position just before the top of the swing was reached, because the golfer was breaking his left wrist down and under the shaft. This wrist maneuver placed the club so that the shaft practically dropped down behind the player at the top of the swing, pointing far to the left of the green or the line of direction. With this truly open position of the club, nothing but slices were produced, of course.

From this extreme open-face handling of the club, there was a tendency to have a reverse weight shift. The weight on the backswing was inclined to shift back to the left foot, and from this kind of footwork, anything but the proper body position resulted.

Learning What's Right. First of all, correct balance at the start of the swing was emphasized. Relationship between the distribution of the weight and the corresponding hand positions was explained, and the player was advised to shift his right hand to a position behind and under the shaft. A necessary relaxing of the tenseness in the grip of the left hand was called for, also.

From the correct starting position, the player was taught to shift his weight to the right foot with the one-two motion. Then, as the club was started from the ball on Step No. 3 of the swing, he learned to use the correct hand action in closing rather than opening the

231. Here is the position of the slicer's club just before the top of the back-swing is reached. The clubface has been thrown open and will probably come through to hit the ball in the same way. Correct hand action can cure this fault. (See Case History No. 4b.)

232. Here I am shown demonstrating one of the causes of a hook shot. Without the correct sequence of movement in the backswing, the player will develop a forward rolling action by the right shoulder in the downswing. With proper footwork and weight shift this movement—which will mean a hook every time—will be corrected. The right body position and hand action will become almost automatic once proper weight shift is learned. (*See Case History No. 5.*)

club, almost immediately creating a new type of swing for him. The club came back in a square or closed position, the weight remained on the right leg as the upswing was completed, and a natural downward pull with the left arm was produced as the weight was reshifted to the left foot, the left side bringing the club down and into the ball.

With this new swing, there was a complete reversal of form for this golfer. From weak, fading, slicing shots, his game became one of crisp, straight shots, with an occasional tendency toward a slight hook. After having been, in effect, a single-arm, one-sided player, he now had learned to use both hands and his entire body in the swing. Golf became fun, rather than work.

Case No. 5—Hooking

This was the case of a man who knew how to get along on his feet. That is, this middle-aged pupil had been quite active in sports other than golf, having played baseball and been a good skater. In golf, however, most of his shots had an annoying tendency to hook. He had good grip and hand position, and he addressed the ball well, with his weight mostly on the left foot and the right knee relaxed as it should be.

Everything looked fine when the player initiated his swing with a forward press. Then, however, instead of making a reverse press and shifting his weight to the right foot before starting the backswing, he immediately did a big, rolling, turn movement with the left arm, left side, and left shoulder. The swing, rather than being a 1-2-3-4 rhythm, was executed with a 1-3-4 series of moves, completely leaving out the key motion in the swing, Step No. 2.

Omitting the correct forward thrust of the left knee on the backswing and the corresponding thrust of the right knee on the downswing, the golfer, through this 1-3-4 rhythm, developed a prominent forward action of the left shoulder in the backswing and a forward rolling action by the right shoulder in the downswing. As a natural consequence of this type of body movement, the left knee flopped toward the right knee on the backswing, and a reverse action took place on the downswing. A wide pronating move by the left arm in the backswing and a similar motion by the right arm in the downswing threw the club into a chronic hooking maneuver every time.

Putting an End to the Hook. By pointing out to this golfer the error of leaving out Step No. 2 in his swing, the author was able to straighten out the hook. Step No. 2 is the reverse press, in which the player shifts his weight to the right foot before the clubhead leaves the ball to start the backswing. When he had learned the proper footwork and weight shift, this player found himself using the correct body position and hand action almost automatically, and he was no longer troubled with his annoying hook.

Case No. 6—Pushing

This case involved a strong young man in his late twenties, a low-handicap golfer, who was having trouble keeping the ball on the line. His shots were not slicing. They just seemed to slide out to the right of the objective on a perfectly straight line, a fault which is called *pushing*.

Making the Analysis. A study of the player's style revealed that he employed the orthodox overlapping grip, a good stance, and a fine position to the ball. There was a good sense of footwork in his swing, with an easy shift of weight to the right foot for the backswing and an equally good reshift to the left foot for the downswing, which gave him a strong, left-side action in the downswing. Further study of the swing revealed, however, that the player's club kept falling into an open position just before the top of the backswing was reached. The left wrist kept breaking down and under the shaft of the club at the top of the swing. This effect was consistent, and observation showed that there was an extremely tense grip with the left hand. In fact, the left hand and arm were definitely in command on the backswing as well as the downswing.

Correcting the Push. The prescription for correcting this fault included a relaxing of the left hand and a slight change of the right

233. Pushing—the ball sliding out to the right on a straight line—can be caused by allowing the club to open just before the top of the swing, and by allowing the left wrist to break down and under the shaft at the top of the swing. (See Case History No. 6.)

hand position from one almost on top of the shaft to one underneath the shaft. Through this change, the player was able to keep his club in a more closed position throughout the swing, and when the already strong left-side action was applied, perfectly straight shots came off his clubs, right on the line.

In this case, the player had excellent footwork and weight shift, good pivot action in the swing, but a decidedly weak position of the club at the top of the backswing, caused by entirely too tense a grip in the left hand. This weakness in the grip made the club come through late under the unusually strong left-side action this player possessed. It was not a matter of reducing the left-side action, but one of building up a good hand action to go with it.

Case No. 7—Pulling

This fault is the reverse of the one just discussed in the previous case. The ball takes off on a straight line to the left of the objective. It does not curve or bend to the left as it does in a hook. The pupil appearing with this error was a youngster in his late teens, a strong player, but constantly troubled by his shots travelling off to the left. His form was good in all respects, except that when he reached the top of the swing he seemed to get stuck at that point and come down and through with the club without reshifting his weight to the left foot. The natural result was an overpowering swing with the right arm, sending the ball off on a straight line, but to the left of the green.

Getting Straightened Out. This pupil was rather tall, and the author noticed that he kept crowding up on the ball and standing more erect than ever. It was suggested that more of a sitting position be adopted, thereby introducing more relaxation in the knees and allowing the weight to be readily shifted to the left foot as well as to the right. Practice and concentration on this weight shift to the left foot as the top of the backswing was reached corrected the bothersome pulling.

234. Pulling is just the reverse of pushing. A pulled ball takes off on a straight line to the left of the objective. Pulling can easily result if the player has a tendency to crowd the ball and to stand erect. Here I am shown in an exaggerated example of this fault. Note, too, that my feet are incorrectly positioned, and that my right hand is too far over on the top of the shaft. *(See Case History No. 7.)*

Case No. 8—The Hooking-Slicing Complex

A teen-age girl with considerable promise as a golfer developed a severe case of smothered hook shots. When asked to play a few shots so that the instructor could see what she was doing wrong, she proceeded to slice six balls in a row, much to her chagrin. Because she had expected to hook her shots, this sudden burst of slices proved embarrassing, and she confessed that she could find no solution for correcting either fault.

Locating the Trouble. It was observed that her placement of the hands on the club was good, but she addressed the ball with her left knee relaxed and her right knee fairly straight. This put most of her weight on the right foot at the start of the swing. As a matter of fact, she actually was part of the way into her swing, because she was already turned slightly to the right. With her body in this position, it was impossible to use body pivot as a means of swinging the club away from the ball. About the only thing she could do was to pick the club straight up with the left hand, and this is exactly what she did, naturally rolling the arm and the club into an open position at the same time. When she reached the top of the swing, the only thing she could do was to drive forward as hard as she could with her right hand. This resulted in a terrific roll-over action with the clubhead, causing a smothered hook shot, which to my way of thinking is the most sickening shot in golf. The slice, although it may not travel far, at least flies in the air for a while, anyway.

Extreme tension in the first few shots caused this girl to leave the club in an open position as she came through. This caused the slices that she did not understand. After relaxing a bit, however, she soon got the right hand working on the downswing and went into her usual hook routine. This girl could not hit a straight shot except by accident. She sliced or hooked the ball almost every time. Asked if she had ever heard of the term *forward press,* she replied that she had not. She had heard about pivoting, but had never been told about footwork or weight shift.

235. "Throwing" the club at the ball can mean a hook or a slice. Shown here is the roll-over action of the clubhead that causes a smothered hook shot. This fault will not happen if footwork and pivot are correct, for then the hands will not merely swing the club but will be free to steady and guide it. (See Case History No. 8.)

Basic Training. It was explained to this pupil that all the power in a golf shot comes from the pivot motion of the body. She learned that there are two pivots in a golf shot, a turn of the body on the right leg for the backswing and a turn on the left leg for the downswing. Before there can be pivot, she was told, there must be weight shift. When the weight shift operation is executed, the pivot motion becomes easy and natural. When pivot is established, the hands are free to exert control and guidance over the club position.

The pupil found that she (1) had no idea of correct footwork and weight shift, (2) could not pivot properly because of this, and (3) was trying to swing the club with the hands, when they should have been free to steady and guide the club.

Learning Her Lessons. It was necessary for this golf student to start way back at the beginning, learning how to get the club, her body, her weight, her hands, and her feet lined up correctly. This was accomplished very easily by following the first set of 1-2-3-4 steps, the method of assuming the position for starting the swing. As part of *Lesson No. 1,* she was shown the one-two process of shifting the weight from the left foot to the right foot, and the three-four method of using the body to raise the club to the top of the swing and bring it down and through the ball. With a little practice, some fine shots were made in this first session.

The same procedure was followed in *Lesson No. 2*—the 1-2-3-4 method of getting the club, the feet, the hands, and the body lined up for the swing, and the second 1-2-3-4 rhythm of weight shift and body action to execute the swing.

When the girl appeared for *Lesson No. 3,* she reported that she had surprised herself with some of the shots she had made in practice, for she had never hit a ball that well before. Through footwork and body pivot, she was getting into a position at the top of the swing in which she could come down and through the ball with her left side and left arm. Previously, she was forced to "throw" the club at the ball with her right hand. In this third lesson, the method of using the hands to guide and steer the club at the outset of the backswing was demonstrated, and the pupil immediately grasped the reasoning behind it and began to use it effectively.

The pupil's lessons were spaced about a week apart, and she practiced two or three hours between each lesson. By the time she took *Lesson No. 4,* she had completely organized footwork, hand action, and pivot into a smooth-flowing action, with the result that a 200-yard carry with a No. 3 wood was a comparatively simple matter. Before very long, she was making some remarkable scores, and she has won some important tournaments.

Case No. 9—Hooking and Slicing Again

In this instance, a man who had been playing golf for years came to me for help. He could use his irons fairly well, but not without hooking continuously, and the woods were of no value to him because he couldn't get anything but shots that popped right up into the air.

Doing It Wrong. Examination of this player's style showed that he assumed an extreme sitting type of position to the ball, with the weight evenly divided on both feet. There was no effort made to shift the weight, and consequently there was no pivot or body turn. The only thing this player could do was to raise the club with the left arm and return it to the ball with the right arm. This usually resulted in low, sickening, smothered hooks bent off the clubs. It was almost an identical situation with that of the girl in Case No. 8 —no weight shift, no pivot, no positive control of club position with the hands. There was but one thing to do—make a completely fresh start to build into this golfer's swing the operations he was leaving out.

Righting the Wrongs. The pupil was put through the organized routine of relearning the golf swing. He was taught (a) the correct set-up of club, feet, hands, and body, (b) the importance of weight shift and the correct manner of carrying out the moves involved in it, (c) how to employ the body as a means of motivating the club

236. Hooking and slicing are faults that are usually fairly easy to correct—but the problem is to find the cause of the fault. In this drawing I am shown in an extreme sitting type of position that some golfers take when addressing the ball. A position such as this can result in sickening smothered hooks. (See Case History No. 9.)

237. Shanking has been called the most frustrating golfing fault. With little or no weight shift, the left shoulder and left side will carry the club in a low position as it is brought back. (See Case History No. 10.)

in the pivot, and (d) the method of using the hands to guide and control the club.

All of these factors were coordinated in a very short time through the use of the first 1-2-3-4 method of preparing for the swing and the second set of four steps for carrying out the swing with the proper footwork, pivot, and hand action. This golfer earned a new lease on his golf game shortly thereafter by scoring a surprise win in a tournament.

Case No. 10–Shanking

Of all golfing faults, shanking undoubtedly is the most frustrating, because the ball just squirts off the club. But shanking can be corrected, just as any other golf fault, and it can be done without resorting to specially-made clubs or specially-designed swings. Shanking, because it is a more advanced type of golfing error, may require more than average treatment, but it can be conquered.

In the case we will describe here, the player had played golf for years, not too well, but well enough to enjoy the game at a handicap of 18. Suddenly, he started shanking his shots. Soon the habit became quite regular, and his golfing pals gave him no relief! In a short time, he found it difficult even to complete certain holes, and he was on the verge of giving up the game.

Discovering the Trouble. Analysis of this player's technique revealed that he used the interlocking grip incorrectly, and this was a great part of his trouble. Some of our top-notch champions use the interlocking grip very effectively, but our pupil employed it in a manner that developed an unusually tight grip with the last three fingers of the left hand. The club practically was locked or frozen in the back of the left hand, and the player had to start the club from the ball with an extreme pronating movement of the left forearm.

There was no weight shift, so the left shoulder and left side went into the backswing carrying the club to a low position as it was brought back. This left-side turn caused the weight to tip back to the left foot during the backswing. Here was the player's position

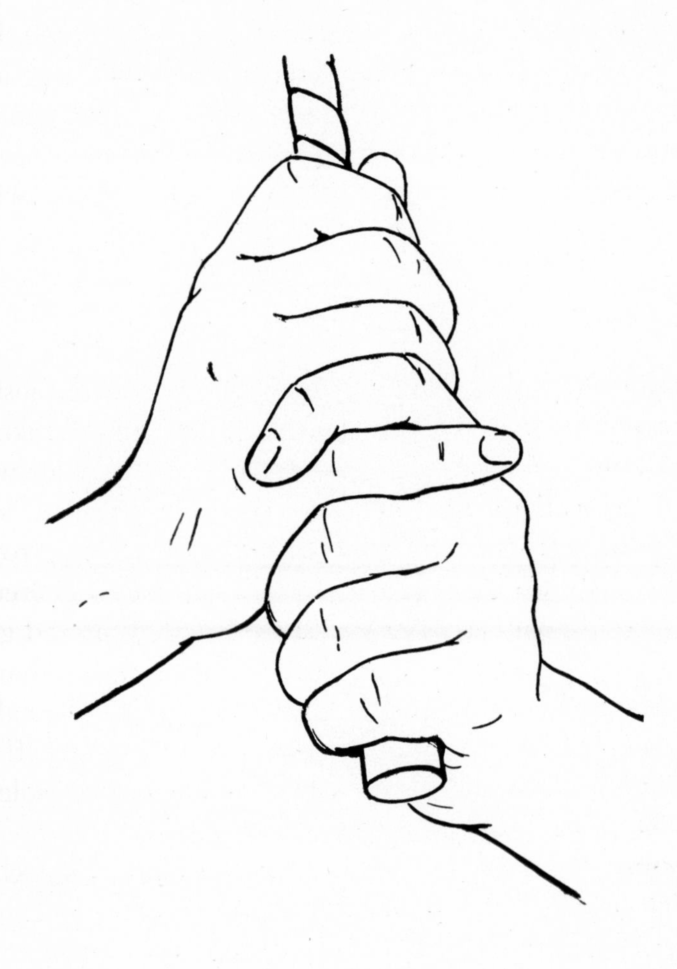

238. The interlocking grip as seen from below shows the little finger of the right hand interlocking with the first finger of the left hand. This type of grip is very popular with many professionals, but it can be used incorrectly—that is, with too tight a grip with the last three fingers of the left hand. (See Case History No. 10.)

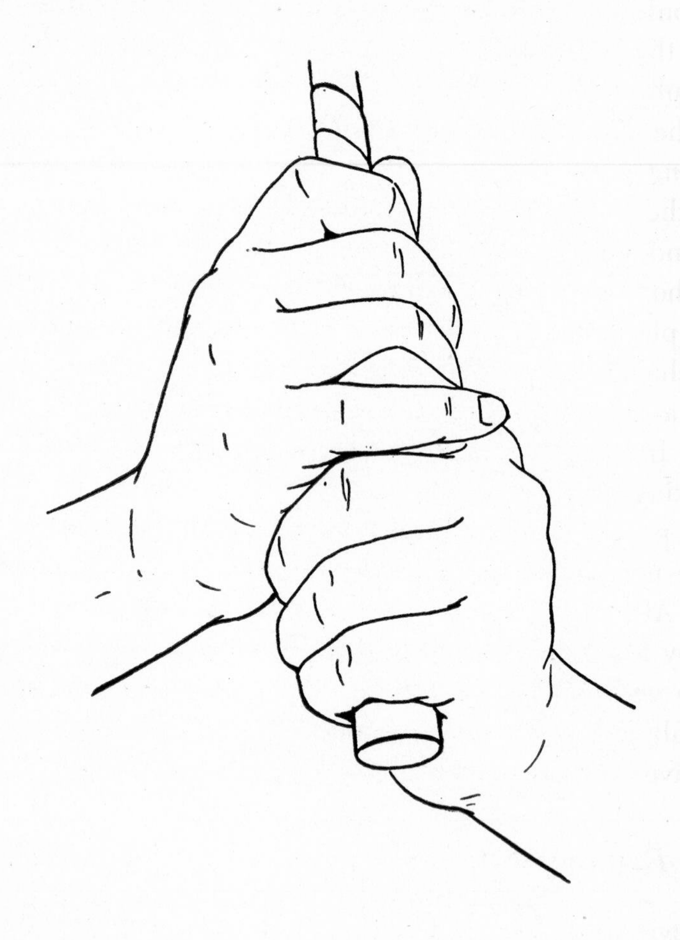

239. The most popular grip is the overlapping grip, in which the little finger of the right hand laps over the forefinger of the left hand. It has an advantage in that the right hand is slightly under the shaft of the club. (See Case History No. 10.)

at the top of the swing—club wide open, left hand tight and left wrist turned under the shaft, weight listed back to the left foot.

The only swing the golfer could make from this position was one bringing the club out and then across the ball. About the only part of the club which could contact the ball was the heel, because the face of the club was too open to ever come in contact.

Making Some Changes. The first thing that was done was to change the pupil's grip from interlocking to overlapping, with the right hand placed well under the shaft. By employing the one-two method of footwork, the weight was shifted to the right foot in the first phase of the backswing. This enabled the player to completely change the position of the club from the extreme open position to a square or closed one. Almost immediately, his shots changed from shanks to slices to straight shots, with an occasional hook taking place.

This pupil's scores dropped from 110 to 100, then to 90, and they are now down in the 80's. So don't get discouraged if you shank. After all, a shank is nothing but an exaggerated slice produced by too much tension in the left hand, a factor which throws the club wide open, and lack of pivot. Analyze your next shank. It undoubtedly will occur on some short shot to the green when you fail to pivot and have a death grip with the left hand.

On the Eighteenth Hole

A review of the preceding typical case problems shows that there are three basic check points in each case we have described. The first is footwork, through which correct body turn or pivot is possible. Body pivot is the second, and it provides the power or energy to swing the club. The third is hand action, probably the most important of the three, for the hands impart the generated power to the club and determine the manner and angle at which the club meets the ball. While these three points are the main ones, it should be remembered that stance influences body pivot and grip influences the working of the hands.

Using the Formula. The basic formula for good golf is:

1. Learn to use the body as the means of providing power and swinging the club.
2. This leaves the hands free to impart this power to the club, at the same time controlling and determining club position throughout the swing.

Application of this formula made it possible to rectify all of the problems encountered in the preceding cases. There was a basic form to which the player was supposed to conform. Did he have the correct body pivot? If not, why not? If he had the correct pivot, did he respond or cooperate properly with the hands?

Although it may have been a faulty stance or an incorrect grip that was the primary cause of the problem, in many cases the players lacked a basic outline or plan of action in making the golf swing. In the author's many years of teaching golf, he has never found a pupil who did not get natural, easy results through application of the form described in this book, once the pattern was understood.

Straight Left Arm? From time to time, pupils have asked about the reason for my refusal to insist upon a straight left arm in the swing. Through teaching experience, I have learned that only certain individuals actually can maintain a straight left arm throughout the swing. Most golfers find it awkward to attempt this. It is true that as the club is being brought to the top of the swing there is a natural extension or straightening of the left arm. However, this is a *natural* straightness, and it is the mark, not the cause, of a good player. In no case is it necessary to cultivate a stiffness or rigidity in the left arm.

Three Little Words

As a means of breaking up faulty golf habits and portraying the necessary motions, I have employed three words—*akimbo, pronate,* and *groove*—and they have been a great aid to me.

I remember *akimbo* as a word used in Washington Irving's *The*

Legend of Sleepy Hollow, which we read in the fourth grade. It described the manner in which Ichabod Crane, the lanky schoolmaster, held his arms when seated on a donkey which was much too small for a man of his height. Crane's arms were akimbo, elbows pointed outward, and that is the position all good golfers assume when they get ready to start the swing. This akimbo position automatically develops a natural sense of relation throughout the arms, tending to prevent a tense, tight grip with the left hand. It also makes it comfortable and easy to start the forward press and facilitates the shift of weight to the right foot at the beginning of the backswing.

Pronate is a term indicating the movement of the hands and forearms. It is helpful in explaining the action of the left hand, through which the position of the club is determined at the outset of the backswing. If the forearm and the left hand turn in the direction of the thumb, this is a pronating movement. When this movement occurs on the backswing, the club is thrown into an open position, and the player can expect a slice to take place. If the forearm and hand are kept steady or turned away from the thumb, this motion is called *supination,* the opposite of pronation. This puts the club in a closed position, which is the position necessary for good, strong shots in golf, and the one that is needed to produce a hook. As the reader can see, *pronate* and *supinate* are words that explain the action of the left hand in regulating the club on the backswing.

The useful word *groove* effectively describes the pattern of the movement of the golf club in the backswing and the downswing, the arc of the swing. Very few golfers seem to realize that the club does not go back and forth on exactly the same line. Because the golfer shifts his weight to the right foot for the backswing and pivots on the right leg, and then reshifts his weight to pivot on the left leg for the downswing, he is using one axis for the backswing and another for the downswing. Consequently, the path or groove of the swing changes slightly as it comes down and through the ball.

Some years ago, when the path of Bobby Jones' club was charted through the use of a camera with an extra fast shutter, this change of groove or arc became apparent. It was announced that the wonderful swing of the world champion had a flaw in it. If that is a flaw, Snead, Nelson, Burke, and the other golfing greats all have it, and they're doing all right.

One final word—

> *A round of golf a week,*
> *Regardless of the score,*
> *Will do more good than a ton of pills*
> *Or an ocean of medicine!*

The Eight Steps

The following pages contain an analysis in outline form of the eight steps that constitute the Novak system of how to put power and direction in your golf.

The First Half:

How to do it

STEP 1

Place Club to Ball

Do this with left hand. Be sure club shaft is tilted forward so that left hand is over a point ahead of the ball. Left hand on top of shaft—three knuckles in view of player. V pointing towards right shoulder.

STEP 2

Adjust Feet

Left heel opposite the ball. Toes on a line parallel to line of shot. Weight even on both feet.

STEP 3

Relax Right Knee to Complete Grip

In order to bring right hand to the club, right knee must be relaxed. This shifts weight over to the left foot and brings hand to the club in natural manner so hand is squarely behind shaft in sort of "slapping" position. Right hand (more under shaft than on top) is directly opposite left hand, so when one "pulls" the other hand "pushes." Balance of club or grip confined solely to first two fingers and thumb of each hand. This permits free movement of club.

STEP 4

Turn Right Heel Out

This outward turn of right heel moves foot from normal position of having toe pointed slightly outward to that of having right foot at right angle to line of shot, or even slightly "pigeon-toed."

Taking Position

Purpose	*Result*
This gives feel and sense of aim with the club.	
This confirms "aim" by aligning body properly.	
This move is most important. It gives proper "feel" of club in hands and yet this can't be done without proper adjustment of weight and body position. In effect, it brings body, weight and hands together in coordinated relation to the club.	This series of moves teaches player to assume automatically the proper position to make the stroke. It provides a coordination of foot, body, weight and hand position which properly balances or poises the player for the swing while at the same time player gets feel of direction and feel of club. When the four moves are completed player is balanced with weight on left foot.
This gives more secure right foot position which is essential because one must be steady on right foot at top of swing. This move also relaxes right hip position so that full free turn to right can be made on upswing.	

The Second Half:

How to do it

As the player is ready to start the swing, right knee is slightly relaxed and weight is on left foot, but left knee is not straight or locked. To start, right knee is bent forward even more (this is one of two moves of knee action necessary to shift the weight). This action is so common with good golfers that it has acquired a name and it is known as *"the forward press."* This action swings or rocks the club shaft forward.

STEP 1

Forward Press

After the forward press of the right knee is made, it is possible to change or reverse the knee position, and, as the knees change position [right knee straightens (but not to a point of locking) and left knee relaxes and bends forward], the weight changes or shifts to the right foot. This, of course, is necessary so that player can turn body and swing club to the right. Clubhead remains on ground but hands and club handle rock over to the right and at conclusion of the move, hands are almost opposite right knee.

STEP 2

Reverse Press

The Swing

Why

As position is taken to the ball, player will find his weight shifted to the left foot, as it should be. However, player wants to swing or carry club to the right. This is impossible while weight is on the left foot, so a change of knee position must be made whereby weight is transferred to the right foot. This is the first of two moves in knee action necessary to shift the weight from left foot to the right foot.

If a person is standing erect with feet close together, weight will be evenly divided on both feet. When one knee is relaxed or bent forward, weight automatically goes to the opposite foot. This process of relaxing one knee and straightening the other is the natural way to shift the weight from one foot to the other and back and forth as desired.

Warning: Do not exaggerate this knee action, as weight then goes to wrong foot. That is why good golfers work their knees in such a modified way that the uninformed are not aware of the knee action.

Caution: While hands rock forward on Step 1 and backward on Step 2, be sure that feet remain on the ground. On Step 3 left heel is raised and on Step 4 right heel is raised; but keep heels on ground during Steps 1 and 2.

The Second Half:
(Continued)

How to do it

STEP 3

Start Club with the Right Hand

As the preceding move is completed, hands are rocked over to the right and at this point the club is really thrown into control of right hand. This pick-up action will develop a countering downward thrust on part of left hand. The downward thrust of left hand positions or cocks the club as desired. The hands, with the pick-up action of the right and the downward thrust of the left, actually immobilize each other so that the only recourse the player now has is that of turning the body to the right and thereby swinging the club up and away with a body turn or pivot.

STEP 4

Swing Through

When weight was shifted to right foot and right hand initiated the movement on the club that induced countering or downward thrust action in left hand, the hands nullified each other against any further movement. Only thing player can do now is reshift weight to left foot and swing club through with a reverse turn of the body.

The Swing
(Continued)

Why

Hands and body work together to swing the club up and away from the ball. The action originates in the right hand, develops counterwise in the left hand and arm which actions position the arms perfectly—the right one bent and close to the right side of body and the left one becoming naturally but comfortably straight. In this position of natural opposition wherein neither arm can move, the only alternative is to set up a turn of the body to the right.

[Club is positioned or cocked with the hands so that direction and character of shot are thereby determined. This further forces player to use body turn to swing club back and forth, which is the natural way to swing the club. (All done in a natural sequence, yet almost simultaneously.) Can be practiced separately and eventually done together.]

As explained under "How to do it," only thing player can do is to reshift weight to left foot and swing club down and through with a reverse turn of the body. This motion is centrifugal action whereby one truly swings from the "inside out," in a full free "follow through."

INDEX

Index